CH00666519

Lionel Robinson was
Aunt Viola's father (Jean Jack's wife
Humphrey Evans (my godfather) was
his grandfather. Mrs Robinson lived
on to the 1950's

Lionel Robinson
Cricket at Old Buckenham

Stephen Musk

Front cover: Lionel Robinson in the grounds of Old Buckenham Hall (Ian MacLaren album, courtesy of Michael Down).

Back cover: Lionel Robinson, from his 1922 Scotch Collegian obituary; and Old Buckenham Hall Ground 100 years on with modern pavilion and electronic scoreboard. Lionel's rustic thatched pavilion was to the right where the nets now stand. (Tom Walshe)

First published in Great Britain by
Association of Cricket Statisticians and Historians
Cardiff CF11 9XR.
© ACS, 2014

Stephen Musk has asserted his right under the Copyright, Designs and Patents Act 1988 to be identified as the author of this work.

British Library Cataloguing-in-Publication Data.
A catalogue record for this book is available from the British Library.

ISBN: 978 1 908165 52 7
Typeset and printed by The City Press Leeds Ltd

Contents

Foreword by Tom Walshe

'Distinguished by his industry and integrity. His sense of justice and kindness of heart endeared him to all.' Those defining words on the life of Lionel George Robinson speak to us down the years from his memorial in the picturesque parish church of All Saints at Old Buckenham in Norfolk. But is the epitaph justified? Can this be the man variously described by writers over the years as 'a strange character' who was 'obstinate and aggressive' and even 'a vulgar Philistine'?

It is indisputable that the Australian financier and sportsman left indelible marks on the history of Anglo-Australian commerce, cricket and horse-racing. He may have carved himself only a small niche in English society, but he made a big impression on the London Stock Exchange, became a significant figure in the annals of the Turf, and, at Old Buckenham in 1921, staged one of the most fascinating, idiosyncratic cricket matches of the age, a so-called private Test match between England and Australia.

Has Robby (his nickname may help 'endear him to all') had an undeserved bad press? Literary and newspaper references in the past 30 years have tended to draw on an article published in the *Sunday Times* in 1977 whose author, Barry Wilson, asserted that Robinson failed in his ambition to gain acceptance as one of the gentry and, even more damning, that 'as a country gentleman he was neither genteel, effortless nor stylish. He was obstinate and aggressive and known for his abusive slanging matches with staff.'

In this volume, Stephen Musk offers a far more reasoned and rounded picture of Robby's complex character. Vain, quick-tempered and ostentatious he may have been, but he was also loyal and generous, a noted benefactor, and a devoted family man whose kindness of heart might have only been apparent to those closest to him.

This is essentially a cricket book, however, for Lionel Robinson's most enduring and evocative legacy stems from his role in the game's pre-1914 'golden age' and its slow renaissance following the dereliction wreaked by the Great War. Here, also, is a fascinating account of Robby's association with Archie MacLaren, former England captain and icon of cricket-lovers in both England and Australia, whose twilight years in the game were largely spent organising and participating in country house matches at Old Buckenham. Stephen has meticulously traced long-forgotten fixtures and performances to provide a window on an amazing panorama of cricket, ranging from the rustic to the regal, that the swashbuckling Aussie and his right-hand Englishman brought to an unassuming East Anglian village.

Tantalising questions remain, of course. The what-might-have-been conjecture centres on 1912, a significant year in Robinson's cricket odyssey. He had finished building Old Buckenham Hall and his nearby racing stud, was at the height of his financial powers, and his pristine new cricket ground beside the hall was complete and ready for use with MacLaren installed as his cricket manager. It was also the year of the ground-breaking Triangular series when both Australia and South Africa toured England. Was this an opportunity for Robby to become something more than a bastion of country house cricket? Did he covet a part on the bigger stage? He had the money to make an impact; the tie-up with MacLaren added credibility.

Cricket had no commercial sponsors in those days, so the money required to guarantee an international side's participation (and provide a few extras to oil the wheels of the tour) had to be raised from private sources. Step forward L.G. Robinson as a guarantor for the South African tourists, including an early invitation for team members to spend a weekend of relaxation and exercise at Old Buckenham. He may well have also sponsored the Australians, though evidence has proved elusive.

Robinson demonstrated he could be relied on get a top cricket show on the road, but it was apparently not enough to win him power or influence within the hierarchy of cricket's snooty establishment. Perhaps he was a bit too brass-necked, a bit too Australian, to be handed a bigger role in the English game. There was to be no MCC membership, no place at the top table. Then the war put a tin hat on it all anyway, and it was not until cricket emerged from those darkest of times that Robinson and MacLaren came to prominence again.

The 1921 match between a strong England team, playing as L.Robinson's XI and captained by MacLaren, and the formidable Australian tourists led by Warwick Armstrong was to prove Robby's final hurrah. Already suffering from terminal cancer, he declined inexorably during the early months of 1922 and died in July aged just 55.

Cricket lived on at the hall ground, however, though without the international players who had graced Robby's arena. The author continues the story to cover the colourful tenure of bon viveur playboy Everard Gates, whose father bought the estate from the Robinson family. As Gates' lifestyle increasingly impacted on his wealth, the hall estate and the cricket ground entered a moribund era in the 1930s. Here, with the cricketing hiatus, Stephen Musk's fascinating story comes to a natural conclusion.

The decline of Lionel Robinson's beloved hall and cricket ground – testimonies to the alliance of 'new money' with Edwardian grandeur – was temporarily arrested by the establishment of a private prep school in Robby's grand house just before the Second World War. It proved a short-lived reprieve, though, as fire ravaged the building in December 1952, removing Old Buckenham Hall School from the village and plunging the cricket ground back into a state of neglect. For a while it was a campsite, its boundaries skirted by an ugly motorcycle grass-track.

By 1960 the once carefully manicured turf had become an unkempt hayfield. An annexe of the hall that survived the fire was the home of engineer Oliver Sear, whose sporting interest was motor racing rather than cricket (he was one of the founders of the Snetterton circuit). However, as local farmer Ernie Panks harvested the annual hay crop from the outfield, his chance remark, 'wouldn't it be nice to see cricket played here again', received a favourable response from Sear who invited the village team back to its rightful home. It has been there ever since, rising through the ranks of local cricket with the benefit of one of the finest grounds in Norfolk which is nowadays increasingly used as a venue for representative matches.

Introduction

It would be a cliché to say that Lionel Robinson is a 'forgotten man' of Norfolk cricket but it would also be true for, even during the few years when teams bearing his name were playing in matches deemed to be of first-class status, he himself was a shadowy figure to natives of his adoptive county. Contemporary reports in the Norfolk press might have gone into considerable detail about the deeds of 'Lionel Robinson's XI' at his ground at Old Buckenham Hall but they had little to say regarding the man himself.

Nor has history deigned to redress the balance and give Robinson due credit for his achievements. Although the first first-class game granted to him saw his eleven defeat the 1912 South African tourists by no fewer than 191 runs, he is now remembered almost solely for attracting the 1921 Australians to Old Buckenham Hall to play against what was a near-Test strength eleven captained by his cricket manager, Archie MacLaren. Writers who have covered this match in any detail have tended to fall into two categories: those concerning themselves with the deeds of the formidable tourists, and those detailing the Indian summer of the first-class career of MacLaren. None has been particularly interested in the man whose money and vision had made the game possible (with the honourable exception of Jeremy Malies who, ironically, has the least space available in which to digress on Lionel) whilst one, Ronald Mason, almost rejoices in his ignorance of Robinson – presumably to cover-up his lamentable failure to do any research.

Many of those who know a little about Lionel Robinson are likely to agree broadly with the popular but rather implausible hypothesis advanced in 'The Cricketer Book Of Cricket Eccentrics And Eccentric Behaviour' (edited by Christopher Martin-Jenkins). This states that: 'Lionel Robinson's dream was to host a match at his own country house between England and Australia. First though, he had to find a house .... He was attracted by a manor house at Old Buckenham, some 15 miles south-west of Norwich .... He bought it and completely restyled it. He appointed Archie MacLaren, the former Lancashire and England captain, as his manager .... to [Robinson's] delight he was able to persuade the Australians to play the second match of their 1921 tour on *his* ground.' This strikes one as unsatisfactory on at least three points. First, although Lionel had been a keen spectator at the Melbourne Cricket Ground, there is absolutely no evidence whatsoever that he was actively involved in cricket before he was settled in Old Buckenham; indeed it is more than likely that his interest was kindled by the activities of the village club after he became lord of the manor. Second, Old Buckenham would have been a wilfully remote choice of venue for someone who was driven by a life-long goal to host high quality cricket; although it was still an age in which elevens raised by wealthy or prestigious individuals might secure fixtures against touring sides, these were usually played at established venues with reasonable links to public transport, not in a remote, tiny village in the middle of the countryside of a minor county which was itself geographically isolated. Much more likely is the theory advanced in chapter three that Lionel and his business partner, Bill Clark, bought the estate at Old Buckenham with the primary purpose of setting up their stud farm, which was well-sited to interact with the headquarters of British racing at Newmarket and that Lionel's cricket began as a sideshow. Third, it assumes that, when Robinson's attention was finally turned to high quality cricket, his goal was solely to attract a visit to Old Buckenham by an Australian touring eleven and fails to consider the hypothesis presented in the foreword by Tom Walshe that he had bigger fish to fry and may have wished to become a significant mover-and-shaker in the world of English cricket.

Whilst the facts about Lionel's intention to rub shoulders with the MCC in the corridors of power may never be fully discovered, the truth, that there was no grand, long-term plan can be found tucked away in an article entitled "Country House Cricket", published in *The Cricketer* in 1932. Written by Evelyn Metcalfe, who played frequently for Robinson's teams, it makes it clear that Robinson was already installed as lord of the manor in Old Buckenham and was busy encouraging the village team when Metcalfe himself suggested that he should have a "good cricket ground" created on the estate[1]. Even then, the prospect of attracting visiting tourists of Test status does not seem to have arisen immediately, growing instead out of Robinson's success as an extremely generous host of country house matches. Cricketers from the dominions were made especially welcome at these; one source stating that 'there are many Australian cricketers who will remember as one of the outstanding events of their tour of this country the fine hospitality they enjoyed at Old Buckenham Hall, where Lionel Robinson loved to entertain them'.

Lionel himself was a player of extremely limited ability[2] and was happy to play for the village side (he batted in the 'tail' and did not bowl), and his take-over of cricket in Old Buckenham was a gradual affair; he brought in both cricketers of note and also cronies of his from the world of finance who had some cricketing ability and the locals were frozen out when Robinson took Metcalfe's advice and funded the construction of his splendid new ground; the villagers had to continue playing on their old ground and their team disappears from view in 1912. (Ironically, Robinson also froze himself out as a player for, although he was just about worth his weight as a village cricketer, he was not good enough to play in his own elevens.) A good deal of confusion in the nomenclature of the elevens playing under Robinson's name (see Appendix) has obscured the picture but the basic facts are clear: within three years of playing village cricket

---

1   Metcalfe was so keen to take credit for the concept of Lionel's ground that he repeated his claim in The Cricketer more or less word-for-word ten years later.

2   The Cricketer puts it bluntly, stating that: "he never gained any fame as a player..."

(and poor village cricket at that) Lionel was hosting a succession of high-quality country house games building up to his crushing defeat of the South African tourists. Martin-Jenkins' hypothesis is again shown to be inaccurate by the fact that Robinson had played a leading role in inviting the Australian tourists to Norfolk in 1912 for a match against an England XI at the County Ground at Lakenham[3]. It seems clear that Lionel was one of the financial guarantors for the Lakenham match and he definitely acted as host to several of the English amateurs who were selected to play in this fixture[4]. These were not the actions of a man whose life-long goal was being thwarted before his very eyes but those of a man playing a longer game, with his eyes on the chance to exercise real power. It is highly unlikely that Robinson would have regarded the visit to Old Buckenham a few days later of the South Africans as a consolation prize, as the view of Martin-Jenkins would suggest[5]. To attract <u>any</u> tourists to his private ground so early in its existence was, in reality, a great personal coup and Robinson's own thoughts on this matter, which may have been mixed and complex, will remain forever unknown.

This volume aims to chart in detail the rise of 'Lionel Robinson's XI' beyond the game of 1912, on to the Great War, which very nearly brought Robinson's ambitions to an end. Although the village club sprang back to life after the Great War, even being permitted to play on Robinson's ground and thriving as never before, Robinson only just managed to keep top-quality cricket at Old Buckenham alive until the 1921 season when the Australian tourists visited Old Buckenham and Lionel finally got his main wish. Perhaps fittingly, he died not much more than a year afterwards; it is a little known fact that he had been suffering from cancer for several years and this might explain his inactivity after the war, relative to the busy programme of matches over which he presided between 1910 and 1914. Robinson's interests outside of cricket will be dealt with, such as his extremely lucrative business career, the rebuilding of the estate and the development of the successful stud farm. The fate of his descendants will also be charted to show that, while Robinson himself might have been irredeemably 'new money', his family did find acceptance within England's nobility. Finally the continued flourishing of cricket at Old Buckenham after Robinson's death will be detailed.

Given his almost complete lack of ability as a player and the short-lived, even ephemeral, existence of his cricket teams, the sceptic might ask why Robinson is worth remembering at all. The first five of his first-class matches are of little historical importance except to the fanatic (although that victory over the 1912 South Africans made for an impressive debut).

---

3   1912 was the year of the Triangular Tournament with both the South Africans and the Australian touring Britain.

4   Australian sources stress the importance of Lionel's role in organising this match, one even stating that the: "England eleven...was got together by Mr Lionel Robinson"

5   Robinson was actually named as being one of the financial guarantors of the South African tour and, before the players officially began their season, was happy to host a weekend party which no fewer than eight of the South African squad attended. Also present was Claude Jennings, the vice-captain of the Australian team who had arrived in England earlier than his team-mates.

It is in the final first-class game that Robinson's team took its place centre-stage in the history of cricket. After the Australian tourists of 1921 got their noses bloodied at Old Buckenham, MacLaren went on to captain the England XI which finally lowered the colours of the previously invincible tourists at Eastbourne. The link between the two games was nicely covered by Ronald Mason in his book *Warwick Armstrong's Australians* (and I shall be returning to it in chapter six) but, alas, he failed to place the former game in the context of Robinson's endeavours. He granted the host 'a pale minor immortality by association' but stated that 'nobody now remembers [Robinson] at all'. Robinson certainly deserves to be remembered, if only 'by association', and this study aims to ensure that he is not forgotten.

Chapter One:
The early life of Lionel Robinson –
a globetrotter makes his fortune

Ancestors, birth and family

Lionel Robinson's father was Anthony Bennett Robinson JP (1831-1908), who was born at Chilcote in Somerset, the second of four sons[6] of Charles Frederick Robinson (1796-1865), a lieutenant in the Royal Navy, and Eleanor Helyer Rocke (1798-1865). Anthony followed in his father's footsteps at first but then transferred into the mercantile marine. This led to a considerable amount of travelling as he made his way in the shipping trade in the Indian Ocean and the South China Sea. According to his son, William, he first journeyed to Australia in 1853, arriving on 26 November and visiting Melbourne soon after. He kept a detailed diary of this excursion, going into so much detail that he even noted the Bible readings that he made each evening. Anthony also wrote in his diary that he was 'in ecstasy with the grandeur of the Port, the beauty of the splendid country around and the multitude of magnificent vessels anchored around us'.[7] Surviving legal documents have later placed him in Brisbane in the early 1860s and also listed his address in May 1861 as 28 Gordon Street, Gordon Square, Middlesex. Anthony Robinson was residing in Ceylon, now Sri Lanka, when his eldest son, Lionel George Robinson, was born on 29 August 1866 in the Galle Face Hotel, Colombo. The Robinson family moved to Australia when Lionel was only months old.

The story of his mother is of considerable interest; it is glossed over in most sources and I am greatly in debt to Lionel's great-nephew, Michael Robinson, for revealing the truth. She was born Harriet Barton (1840-1910), the seventh out of 12 children (and the fifth daughter) of William (1795-1881) and Mary nee Whydah (1808-1872). Her family were a well-to-do family in Australia, with interests in politics, business and the law;[8] her younger brother was Sir Edmund Barton who trained as a lawyer, entered the NSW parliament and played a leading role in the formation of the

---

6   The third son, Charles John, became Principal of Queens College Harley Street
7   Anthony Robinson arrived in Australia in a time of boom; the discovery of gold near Melbourne in 1851 led to the population of Australia, which had stood at about 500,000 beforehand, more than tripling in the next 18 years.
8   William Barton trained as an accountant in England and emigrated to Australia in 1827 when he was appointed principal accountant and secretary of the Australian Agricultural Company. Backed by wealthy shareholders including directors of the Bank of England and the East India Company and by members of Parliament, Barton's task was to oversee the raising of sheep in NSW on a grand scale. When he travelled out to Australia, he was accompanied by his recently married wife, 25 other passengers, eight French Merino rams and no less than 312 French Merino ewes. When she reached Australia, his wife Mary, who had been well-educated, had time to establish various schools in between her 12 pregnancies.

Commonwealth of Australia in 1901. Fittingly, he became the first Prime Minister of Australia.[9] In 1859 Harriet married Dr Alexander Salmon, by whom she had one surviving daughter; for reasons that remain unclear he decamped *sans* wife to South Africa in 1863-4 and perished in 1866. She travelled to Ceylon where she met Anthony Robinson and they became an 'item' but it remains a mystery why they did not get married in Melbourne until 1869, after the birth of their second son, Frederick Farquhar (1868-1953). In Victorian times 'living under the brush' was very much frowned upon and, if Anthony was as devout a Christian as his son William remembers, it must have been an awkward situation for him morally.[10] Michael hypothesises that proof of Dr Salmon's death might have been hard to obtain and that Harriet was therefore afraid of being jailed as a bigamist before she was absolutely certain of her status as a widow.

Following the eventual celebration of their marriage, which can be said to have 'legitimised' or 'legitimated' young Lionel, Anthony and Harriet had three further sons, and all five were raised in Melbourne. All Anthony's sons achieved prominence in commerce or in public life: apart from Lionel himself, Frederick Farquhar, Gerald Henry (1873-1961) and especially William Sydney (1876-1963)[11] were all successful businessmen while Arthur (1872-1945) became Attorney General for Victoria after a career as a solicitor, often acting for Collins House, and was eventually knighted.

When he finally settled down to family life in Australia, Anthony took a job with the merchant firm of James Henty & Co. before taking up journalism; he wrote on financial matters for the *Daily Telegraph* and the *Herald*. He subsequently became commercial editor of the *Melbourne Age* under A.L. Windsor in 1876, where he was succeeded by his youngest son, W.S., in 1900 (see below).

When Anthony retired, Lionel provided him with a 'family' pension of £250 a year, which allowed his father to live comfortably for the rest of his life. That Lionel was a dutiful, loving son can be seen in the letter dating to March 1897. The reference to 'Ella's grave' relates to his sister, the baby of the family, who had died of typhoid fever the previous year when aged only 18.

Schooling and marriage

Lionel Robinson was educated at Scotch College, Melbourne, between 1879 and 1881. He was a highly promising pupil, winning the prize given by the late Hon Robert Simson for the best scholar in the school under 14 years. In 1880 he was dux of his class, winning a special prize given by Mr E.A.Wynne, but often found himself bested by a contemporary, John Monash, who was later commander of the Australian forces in the Great War. In 1881 he passed his matriculation examination in nine subjects,

---

9   Michael Robinson is in no doubt that Lionel would have capitalised on the political connections of his family when making his way in the business world of the 'old country'.

10 Things might have been made even more awkward by the fact that Salmon's father was a Free Presbyterian minister.

11 William was almost universally known as 'W.S.' and he will be referred to as such.

Letter from Lionel to his parents 1897 showing his dutiful and loving nature as a son (courtesy of Michael Robinson)

taking honours in English. At this point he was obliged to finish his education and take up paid employment for, as his brother Arthur wrote later: 'my father could not afford to keep him at school ... as there were four other hungry boys, who had to be educated, clothed and fed'. There is no evidence of Lionel playing cricket while at Scotch College but when he left he was still too young to be selected for the first eleven and no details of younger cricketers survive.

On leaving, Lionel joined the newly founded Defence Department of the State of Victoria. He soon tired of pen-pushing and found new employment as a clerk with the Melbourne stockbroking company of James Donaldson & Co. He would shortly marry Mary James on 12 March 1890 at St Jude's Anglican church at Carlton in Victoria; she would bear him a son (named Lionel Wyndham), who did not survive infancy, and two daughters, Viola Murielle and Eirene Marguerite, the latter being known in the family as 'Queenie'.[12] His father-in-law was T.R.James, who was head of the Telegraph Department of the Colony of Victoria for many years.

---

12   In 1889 (just prior to his marriage) Lionel had purchased a property in Melbourne, with the address of "Euroma", 2 Beaconsfield Road, which was located in the suburb of Upper Hawthorn. As his younger siblings were still being educated, he was probably unable to receive a financial "leg-up" from his family and had to finance the purchase entirely off his own bat; it remains unclear how he retained ownership of the house when he was declared bankrupt. In March 1897 he transferred ownership of the house to his wife by a Deed of Settlement and she retained possession even after departing the state and the country before selling it to Lionel's brother Frederick in 1906.

Benefactor of Scotch College

In his obituary in *The Scotch Collegian*, Lionel is described as 'one of our greatest benefactors'; his most significant contribution being the establishment of the 'Lionel Robinson' scholarship in 1918. Arranged by his brother, (Sir) Arthur, who was managing Lionel's affairs in Australia by this time, this endowment was sufficiently generous to provide a perpetual fund to pay tuition fees for a bright boy to do what Lionel was unable to do, that is to finish his education with a good chance of obtaining the position of dux of the school. One of the most famous recipients of such funds was (Sir) Zelman Cowen who eventually became Governor General of Australia. Lionel was also one of the first contributors to the fund raised to construct the new Scotch College at Hawthorn Glen; his brother, Arthur, was chairman of the Capital Appeal and would certainly have encouraged him to make a significant donation. [13] On a more informal note, Lionel was praised for his generosity in inviting Old Scotch Collegians to stay with him at Old Buckenham Hall when on leave during the Great War. The most obvious sign of the regard with which Lionel is remembered at Scotch College is a large drinking fountain that has been erected in his honour in the school's main quadrangle.

Making a fortune on the Stock Exchanges

It quickly became apparent that Lionel had the natural flair of a gambler for the stock market and he was lucky in his timing for the boom in the Australian markets that took place in the 1880s enabled him to make significant amounts of money while still very young. He was only 22 when he was able to buy a seat on the Melbourne stock exchange. Lionel formed what turned out to be a life-long partnership with the South Australian-born William Clark (or 'Bill' as he was often referred to in Australian sources)[14] but his career was not one of uninterrupted success; he was actually declared bankrupt in the depression and commercial crisis of 1892-3 and was only readmitted to the stock exchange in June 1893[15]. According to Peter Richardson, the firm of 'Robinson & Clark soon acquired reputations as fearless and successful share market speculators, especially in the field of mining stocks' whilst another writer states: 'One of the most dazzling rises to fortune, made by pure ability and courage, was that of Lionel Robinson and Bill Clark, sharebrokers ... 'Robby' was an

---

13   Arthur Robinson oversaw the purchase of the land for the new school, paying £13,000 British pounds to WL Baillieu, a financier who was already known to Arthur and who would soon become linked to the business careers of all five of the Robinson brothers.

14   William Clark outlived his partner by 26 years but remains a shadowy figure. Between 1921 and 1942 he owned Windlesham Moor, which later found fame as the first family home of Princess Elizabeth and Prince Philip.

15   Michael Robinson informs me that, at this time, many speculators in the fields of finance and real estate ran up huge debts on shares that were only partly paid. Companies that were owed large amounts were often forced to 'bite the bullet' and accept whatever they were able to recover, often only a small fraction of the total amount due. Agreements were often made in secret, leaving those who were technically bankrupt more or less free to start again. Many more prudent folk were highly critical of this practice. There is no evidence that Lionel took advantage of such a scheme except for the fact his return to the financial fray was suspiciously rapid.

1901 census: the Robinson family in Prince Arthur Road, Hampstead.

extremely shrewd operator on the market here and in Adelaide, and he was backed up by 'Bill' Clark, a most sagacious dealer and daring speculator.'

In 1897, the partnership transferred to the Adelaide stock exchange, where the profits to be made speculating in gold mining shares were larger than those in Melbourne and, two years later, Lionel dissolved the partnership and transferred his centre of operation across the globe to England, joining the London Stock Exchange in search of yet more favourable trading conditions. However, Robinson felt the absence of his partner keenly and, after no more than three or four years, made a trip back to Australia in a successful attempt to persuade Clark to join him in London and resurrect their partnership. Within a couple of years, Lionel Robinson, Clark & Co. was the largest broking house in the Australian section of the mining share market and the pair had made a large amount of money, trading aggressively in shares for companies such as the Kalgoorlie gold mine Boulder Deep Levels Ltd. The company also became drawn into the options market and made large profits engaging in agency work for Australian stockbrokers. Before long Robinson, Clark & Co. ceased to be merely a firm of speculators and became more of a finance house dealing largely with the mining industry and offering a wide range of services to prospective clients. They also became, more or less, 'loan sharks', lending large amounts of money at high rates of interest to clients who were not always financially viable; a notorious case being that of Stanley Rowe, whose fraudulent activities were uncovered by Robinson, leading to a ten year jail sentence for the former and the return of a loan of £15,000 to the latter.

Robinson & Clark suffered a setback when the boom in the mining of gold in Western Australia collapsed in 1901-3, and they were forced to diversify[16]

---

16   It has been proposed that they felt obliged to 'clean up their act' after criticisms of their business activities were published. The unfavourable comments were described as 'unsubstantiated', but it is, perhaps, revealing

but they were again fortunate when a general increase in the price of base metals took place in 1905. This particular boom encouraged Lionel to make a visit to Australia which had extremely important consequences as he and Clark acquired interests in mining companies based at Broken Hill (where silver, lead and zinc were mined) and a rather informal, but extremely influential, group called the Anglo-Australian Group came into being. According to his brother, W.S.: 'Between these parties there was never any agreement or letter implying any arrangement. They were merely friends believing in Australia and its future.' There was a good deal of financial sleight of hand as companies and syndicates (such as the Hill Syndicate, the Broken Hill Syndicate and the rather shadowy Share Guarantee Syndicate) came and went but there were essentially three major components in this Group; moneyed parties based in both Australia and in England and a group of technical and administrative experts. The major providers of capital and financial services in Australia were the Baillieu brothers William Lawrence ('W.L.'), Edward Lloyd ('Prince') and Percy Clive ('Joe');[17] the main English backing came from Robinson, Clark and Francis Algernon Govett[18], whilst the chief technocrats were the firm of Bewick, Moreing & Co., for whom the major player was Herbert Clark Hoover, eventually to become President of the USA.

Future United States President Herbert Hoover, pictured in his 30s when a mining engineer and close associate of Lionel at Broken Hill.

During 1905, Lionel organised a trip of potential large-scale investors from Melbourne to the Broken Hill mining fields during which some

---

that, whilst the pair issued justificatory affidavits, they took no direct action against their critics.

17   A descendant of the Baillieu brothers is Ted Baillieu, who was, until 2012, the Premier of Victoria.

18   Govett was born in Surrey in 1858, the son of a stockbroker.

potentially lucrative opportunities were successfully pinpointed by the Group; this resulted in him becoming even more closely associated with some of the other major investors currently active in Australia. One of the major problems concerned the handling of over six million tonnes of sand and slime residue dumps and how best to extract the 12 million dollars of metal, mostly zinc, contained in surface deposits, locally referred to as 'skimp' dumps. The successful solution to this particular problem led to Lionel being one of the founders of the Zinc Corporation Ltd. (ZC) in Melbourne in 1905. A concentrating mill established by ZC was employed to treat material brought in from other mines and the company flourished, soon expanding to diversify into underground operations, cutting back on its treatment of surface residues. In time ZC would be renamed Rio Tinto Zinc, but there were stormy times ahead for that young company in particular and the Anglo-Australian Group in general. Due to a collapse in the share boom at Broken Hill triggered by a stock market panic in New York leading to a sharp fall in the price of base metals, Govett and Hoover, the joint managers of ZC, found the going uncomfortable and the latter became 'very wild' about the share dealings of Lionel and W.L.Baillieu who, he complained, were 'merely market people'. In the long run, however, only those two possessed sufficient capital to rescue the Group and return it to a sound footing. Unsurprisingly, the Baillieu and Robinson families became inextricably linked both financially and socially and the partnership was formalised when Lionel's niece Margaret married W.L.'s son Harry in 1922.[19]

Broken Hill, 1908, the centre of a major financial involvement by Lionel and his associates. (State Records NSW)

19   Bill Clark's daughter, Ruby, had already married WL Baillieu's eldest son, Clive, who later became the 1st Baron Baillieu.

The success of Lionel in developing mining in Australia led to the doors of many a boardroom being opened to him; he lost his reputation as a financial 'wide-boy' and became a respected member of the business community. By the Great War, he and his colleagues in the Group had fingers in many pies; most of Australia's biggest mining companies had one of Robinson's men on the board acting in a managerial capacity. The outbreak of the war more or less brought Lionel's personal business life to an end at the early age of 48, as the markets in mining were severely disrupted and business activities in general were drastically curtailed. After the war, he did not resume activity; if he was not already suffering from the cancer that would see him die in 1922 he had at most a couple of years of relatively good health left to him. He did, however, act as a committee member of the London Stock Exchange from 1915 until June 1921, when he resigned due to his worsening health.

The *Australian Dictionary of Biography* is not being hagiographical when it sums up Lionel's achievements as a stockbroker in both Australia and England as 'extraordinary'. However, his talents in the world of business have tended to be overshadowed by the achievements of his brother, W.S. (see below), who outshone his successes in the long run, his achievements as a racehorse owner and breeder and, in England at least, by his role as a bankroller of high quality country house cricket at Old Buckenham Hall.

William Sydney 'W.S.' Robinson

Although all five Robinson brothers achieved measures of eminence in their professional lives, the career of W.S. outlasted and outshone them all. He showed little enthusiasm for his studies at Carlton, Scotch College and Hawthorn Grammar School but followed his brother, Gerald, through agricultural studies at Longerenong Residential College and joined him on the family fruit farm in 1894. He quickly became disillusioned at the poor prospects and, in 1896, left the farm and joined the *Melbourne Age* newspaper. After an apprenticeship of four years he replaced his father as commercial editor. He was still unsettled, however, and, using contacts that he had made as a journalist, he invested in a struggling knitting mill originally known as Alexander Stewart & Co Ltd; in moving into business he enlisted the help of two of his older brothers - Lionel gave him a loan while Frederick agreed to return from managing a timber company in Western Australia to co-direct the new company. The success of this firm led to the creation of one of Australia's largest textile companies, Yarra Falls Ltd, with Frederick as managing director,[20] while W.S. found himself being drawn into contact with the Baillieu family, both as a professional partner and socially. This contact became closer when Lionel invited W.S. to join that highly significant trip to Broken Hill in 1905. Following two years learning the ropes in studying the business of mining, W.S. was offered a partnership in Lionel's stockbroking company in London.

---

20   Lionel's obituary in the *Times* credited him with helping to finance and develop the textile industry in Australia but this had been small beer for the rich financier; his role was limited to the loaning to W.S. the sum of £2,200 to aid him in the setting up of the Yarra Falls company. His brothers, Frederick, Gerald and W.S., all played more significant roles in that field than Lionel.

*W.S Robinson, Lionel's illustrious brother and business associate
(courtesy of Old Scotch Collegians' Association)*

During the Great War, W.S. worked for the Australian Prime Minister, Billy Hughes, but, when Lionel did not come out of retirement after the war, W.S. resumed business and threw in his lot with his friends and partners in the Baillieu family. Although based in London from 1916, he spent much of his time in Australia and went on to become a businessman and industrialist of global significance. He reached the height of his powers during the Second World War and, in his latter years, helped to establish the Australian aluminium and uranium industries. Unlike Lionel, W.S. was not interested in making money *per se* but was rather motivated to set up and control a worldwide business empire. In his memoirs (which were published posthumously in 1967 and titled *If I Remember Rightly*) he stated, with justification, that: 'I built up...the friendship and goodwill of a great body of workers in Australia and the UK and in the Far East, plus a host of people engaged in finance, commerce and industry in Britain, the Continent, the East and the United States.'[21]

W.S. has been described as 'an imposing but genial figure ...with a disconcertingly mild manner, he could nevertheless exhibit strong temper when crossed'. His death in 1963 made front page news in the Australian press; Lord Chandos, who had been Minister of Production in Churchill's war cabinet, described him as: 'the most completely equipped businessman I have known ... on the broader aspects of economics and monetary thought he had an originality of thought far in advance of his times'.

---

21   In his memoirs, W.S. also remembered both being paid 'the princely sum of a
      gold half sovereign' to wash Lionel's pet hound when a boy and his surprise at
      the severity of the weather in a Norfolk winter when he paid his older brother
      a visit.

Chapter Two:

Robinson comes to Norfolk –
tentative beginnings as a 'rabbit'

Emigrating to England

Although Robinson came to London and joined the Stock Exchange in 1899, he remained closely linked to Australia as a businessman and as an owner of racehorses (see chapter three). It was only after his main coup as a mining industrialist, the trip to Broken Hill in 1905, that he could be said to have settled permanently in England. Before buying Old Buckenham he appears to have been resident in London. The 1901 census shows the Robinson family living at Prince Arthur Road, Hampstead, with Lionel describing himself as 'stockbroker, agent, employer'. Even when he did move to Norfolk, the 1911 census indicates that he maintained a town house in South Audley Street in Mayfair. This might seem to be an appropriate point to consider Lionel's character with a selection of views from those who have gone into print:

Michael Down: 'a strange character' with an 'obstinate, aggressive nature and propensity for abusive slanging matches'.

Jeremy Malies: 'A Philistine of the first chop, [he] was a vulgar if well-intentioned Australian millionaire'.

Barry Wilson: 'Lionel ... tried hard to establish himself as a landed English gentleman ... he had the money but not quite the style ... he was neither genial, effortless nor stylish. He was obstinate and aggressive, and known for his abusive slanging matches with staff.'

Gideon Haigh: he had 'aspirations to enter English society – unsuccessfully ... for he was dismissed as an *arriviste*'.

Leo McKinstry: 'never fully embraced by the establishment because of his aggressive manner'.

Tom Walshe: 'bluff, tough and extremely wealthy ... notoriously obstinate and quick- tempered ... Stories of his irascible nature abounded ... On arriving at Eccles Road station by train from London, he would phone the Hall to demand the entrance gates be opened so he could drive through without hindrance. Once, when his instructions went unheeded, he furiously rammed his car through the gates causing much damage to the vehicle and the obstructing portals.'

Opinions thus seem unanimous that Lionel was very much 'new money' and further evidence that he missed the point of country house cricket is provided both by the inappropriately strong sides that he put in the field to ensure comprehensive victories over unsuspecting visitors and by his behaviour as a spectator at 'his' matches. Many examples of his tendency to put unnecessarily strong sides into the field are given below in chapters three and four – but there is also a 'debunking' of a story, written in *The Cricketer* by Evelyn Metcalfe (supposedly a friendly source) which lampoons Robinson but which is, in fact, a complete fabrication. This might seem to suggest that Lionel was to some extent a victim of his own notoriety; having established a not unearned reputation for poor behaviour, other stories from less reliable sources might well have clung to him (much like they did to Fred Trueman, 50 years later) and made him appear rather more a figure of derision than he merited.[22]

The case for Robinson has been rather swamped by the weight of evidence against him. Tom Walshe describes him as 'a generous host and a loyal, if demanding, employer who fell in love with Old Buckenham and became a respected figure in the village and county'. Reference has already been made in the introduction to his hospitality, especially to cricketers visiting from abroad, and chapter seven will include an account of his funeral, which 'his' villagers attended in droves. A few years earlier, household servants and estate workers had mingled with well-heeled guests at the wedding reception of his daughter Viola at London's Claridges. He may have been a ruthless businessman and no blushing violet, but he was no monster and seemed to inspire affection in those who knew him well. Unsurprisingly, Australian sources are much kinder to their compatriot, one describing him as: 'a good-natured, pleasant man, free of any suggestion of swank'.

Buying and rebuilding the estate at Old Buckenham

The owner of the Old Buckenham estate before Lionel Robinson was Prince Frederick Duleep Singh, who had been resident in Old Buckenham Hall since 1897. He was the second son of the Maharajah Duleep Singh, the King of Punjab, who had six children in all. His father had been deposed by the British authorities while still a minor and brought to England in 1854. Prince Freddy, whose guardian had been Queen Victoria, developed a liking for Norfolk and spent most of his life in the county.

The country house at Old Buckenham was built in Georgian times and Prince Freddy had extensive alterations made. The estate ran to 340 acres and contained stables, pleasure gardens, shrubberies and extensive woodland areas. Within the grounds there were four farms and numerous other smallholdings. He held an annual dinner party for his tenants and also for the owners of adjoining lands which he hired to shoot. He might also have had a cricket ground made at the rear of the hall, but the relation of this shadowy ground to that used by the villagers and to those constructed by Robinson remains unclear.

Prince Freddy seems to have been a perfectionist and was far from happy with the formal gardens that he had laid out, stating in 1904: 'Nothing

---

22   Ironically, Lionel's family can trace their ancestors back as far as the 11th century and so, while Lionel might have behaved as if he was 'new money' he had a very distinguished set of forerunners indeed.

Prince Frederick Duleep Singh's elegant house, demolished to make way for Lionel's mansion (courtesy of Roger Wilson)

goes right, the garden is a failure .... it is disgusting .... people's borders are gorgeous - mine are in swarms'. By 1906 he decided to move on and arranged for the firm of E & H Lumley to sell the estate; they put Old Buckenham Hall up for sale, advertising it as 'A Miniature Mansion in a Miniature Park'.

Lionel duly bought the property[23] but only required the grounds so the fixtures and fittings

were auctioned off separately over as many as four consecutive days in June 1906. A lavish catalogue detailing all 908 lots was published by Pettitt & Cox, titled 'OLD BUCKENHAM HALL CATALOGUE by direction of HH Prince FREDERICK DULEEPSINGH'.

When he made way for Lionel, Prince Freddy did not move far, renting Breckles Cottage, which he renamed 'Breckles House', from Charles Bateman Hanbury. He also spent his final years nearby, residing at Blo Norton Hall which dated from the 16th century and boasted a moat. He died in 1926. Barry Wilson describes Prince Freddy as an 'antiquarian' but states that he is most famous for being the father of the Test cricketer, Kumar Shri Duleepsinhji. Unfortunately there is not a grain of truth in this assertion; Prince Freddy never married and had no issue.

When the estate is referred to in Robinson's times, sources describe it as being around 2,000 acres. Given that Prince Freddy's advertisement described a 'Miniature Park', it is obvious that the great expansion of

---

23   WS, reported in his memoirs that the estate at Old Buckenham had actually passed through the hands of Lionel's ancestors twice before. In the 11th century it had been owned by William d'Albini and in the 15th by Sir John Knyvett. Michael Robinson assumes that it was Lionel who organised for an entry on the Robinson family to appear in Burke's Landed Gentry and for the recognition of their coat of arms and crest for such matters butter no parsnips in Australia.

Old Buckenham Hall, probably pre 1914.
(courtesy of Roger Wilson)

The Dining Room at Old Buckenham Hall.

the estate was due to Robinson rather than his predecessor. He had sumptuous gardens laid out, with first-class facilities for shooting, and created a well-appointed stud farm that survives to this day.

Although Prince Freddy did not exactly live in a hovel, his hall was not grand enough for Lionel. He promptly had the building demolished and, after two new-builds were deemed unsatisfactory and met with a similar fate, finally, by 1911, had completed a mansion which he deemed suitable for a member of the English landed gentry - which is exactly what he aspired to be. The house has been described as either '1930s baroque' or 'neo-Jacobean' in style and contained a magnificent ballroom (part of an enormous entrance hall) and no fewer than 14 bathrooms with all 'mod cons'. Bricks had to be specially imported from the Netherlands to meet Lionel's requirements. It has been estimated that he spent nearly £1m before he was satisfied; to put this in context, when he passed away in 1922 he left just under £250,000 – a goodly sum for that time but an amount dwarfed by that he had spent on his hall.

A glimpse of the grandeur inside the hall was later provided by Allan Sewell, architect son of the headmaster of the school established there in the 1930s.

> 'The Oak Room (was) a beautiful oak-panelled room with a ceiling coved in to form a dome. The windows were leaded in stone mullions in a bay, with a French window in a four-cornered arch. The stone fireplace with its carved over-mantle was flanked either side with fitted bookshelves, drawers and cupboards, also of carved oak. The Dining Room was likewise oak-panelled with a beautiful strap-work ceiling and a stone-surrounded fireplace with a room-height carved oak over mantle in the Corinthian order... The real jewel was the Drawing Room. This was a really lovely room decorated in moulded plasterwork in a rococo Ionic order.... The walnut chimney piece was decorated with swags of fruit and flowers in lime-wood, in the manner of Grinling Gibbons. The centre of the ceiling was a recessed oval with concealed lighting which, combined with candlelight wall brackets, gave the room a lovely subdued light with soft shadows. In the centre of the house was the Grand Staircase, some six or seven feet wide with generous tread and beautifully carved twisted banisters. This was lit from a central light-well by a large mullioned window, each casement with its own stained glass shield.'

The village cricket club at Old Buckenham

When Lionel Robinson purchased the estate at Old Buckenham there was already a cricket club active in the village which played friendly games against local opposition on Saturdays. It was, however, a far from flourishing club as is clear from the coverage of its matches in the local press. The *Eastern Daily Press* never included its matches in its lists of fixtures published on Saturday mornings and rarely bothered to give the results of games involving Old Buckenham - only four were reported for the whole of the 1908 season. Even when the results were printed, they tended to be 'potted scores' rather than full batting scorecards - only the batsmen's totals were given, not the methods of their dismissals nor the names of the bowlers (and catchers) responsible. This abbreviation is a sure indication that Old Buckenham were bottom feeders in the Norfolk village cricket scene. Nor were they even successful bottom feeders – of the four matches for which results are given, one was drawn whilst three were comprehensively lost. Such was their incompetence that, despite the fact that these were one-day matches, two were lost by an innings (including one to Banham Grammar School, who could hardly have been a fearsome proposition on paper). Furthermore, in the six knocks for which records survive, their highest total was a feeble 71. The only sign that the club had any ambition was in the fact that they put out a junior side on at least two occasions – an unusual move for a small village club in that era – but even the juniors had a disastrous time as they were thrashed in both their games against the youngsters of local rivals Kenninghall, being dismissed for totals of 20, 14 and 19. Perhaps unsurprisingly, no more is heard of a junior side representing Old Buckenham again until 1925 when details of a game against Attleborough Boys were printed in the *Eastern Daily Press*.

The year 1909 proved to be a much rosier season for the village team of Old Buckenham, who won seven and lost eight of the 16 matches that were reported. Indeed, given that the defeats included two games each against Quidenham Parsonage and Quidenham Park, prestigious clubs with 'bragging rights' in that part of Norfolk, this was a much more impressive record than it seems at a cursory glance. Lionel Robinson made his maiden appearance for Old Buckenham in the away game at Kenninghall on 29 May; batting at number eight he contributed eight runs. His contributions to the team's improved fortunes were not particularly noteworthy – he played ten innings in the season, being undefeated twice and scored a mere 49 runs at an average of 6.13 – but did have one moment of triumph when he made the top score (an undefeated knock of 14, batting at number ten)

Evelyn Metcalfe, a teller of tall tales. (Roger Mann)

in the away match against Quidenham Parsonage, whose bowling attack was one of the strongest faced by Old Buckenham all season. The press greeted this triumph as it greeted every single one of Robinson's deeds on the cricket pitch – with complete silence.

The villagers who turned out in 1908 continued to form the nucleus of the team in the subsequent year with names such as R Turner, D Bowen, W Shaw, A Germany, G Gedge, W Groom and various members of the Loveday family all cropping up again and again in the Old Buckenham eleven. Although there would come a time when Lionel Robinson would begin to insinuate 'his' cricketers into the village side, very few of these appeared in 1909. The first to be sighted was the ex-Test player, Gregor MacGregor, who kept wicket against Quidenham Parsonage on 5 June, only a week after Robinson made his debut. One of Lionel's cronies, Evelyn Metcalfe, who later earned fame writing for *The Cricketer*, also made a relatively early appearance on the scene[24] while Cyril Staples (who was barely of first-class status) appeared in the return match with Quidenham Parsonage three weeks later. Lionel also managed to find the occasional place for family and friends; his nephew, Lionel Frederick, made two appearances[25] while two members of the Baillieu family turned out against Long Stratton, presumably while making a social call on their business partner (frustratingly, both are given simply as 'W Baillieu'), but it was only for the last match of the year that Lionel Robinson first flexed his cricketing muscles. The team which lost a two-day match to Dr E.F.Rose's XI by an innings went by the name of 'Mr L Robinson's XI' - the first time that a cricket team was so titled. The vast majority of the team were guests invited by the lord of the manor; however, Lionel had still to develop the habit of packing his team with top-quality cricketers. The only team-members with any first-class experience in his eleven were Maurice Jewell, who would go on to captain Worcestershire but who had made his first-class debut only a couple of months before this game; and Evelyn Metcalfe, whose two first-class games were in an earlier century. The rest of the side are merely names today. Perhaps the magnitude of the defeat set Robinson to pondering on the desirability of recruiting some 'hired guns', whether paid or merely entertained lavishly, that he might challenge the likes of the Quidenhams for those 'bragging rights'.

---

24   Evelyn Metcalfe tells a tale of how he was discomforted when making his first appearance as a cricketer at Old Buckenham. He was staying with Lionel at Whitsuntide and his host suggested that he should take place in a game with the villagers. Metcalfe agreed, donned his I Zingari blazer and proceeded to the village green. Here he found himself in a line-up of 20 cricketers (including the 'village idiot' who was presumably the very same 'Squibs' who will be referred to below) as the carpenter and the blacksmith picked up sides. Much to Lionel's glee, Metcalfe was the last man to be picked. When the carpenter was asked why he hadn't selected the visitor, who would have been comfortably the most accomplished cricketer present he replied: 'I would sooner the devil I know than the devil I don't, no matter what bright colours he may have on.' This tale of cricket that was essentially light-hearted contrasts rather strongly with the serious nature of later cricket at Old Buckenham.

25   In one of the games played by both Lionel and his nephew, four wickets were credited simply to 'Robinson'. Given that there is no evidence that Lionel bowled in any other match, it can be assumed that they were taken by Lionel Frederick.

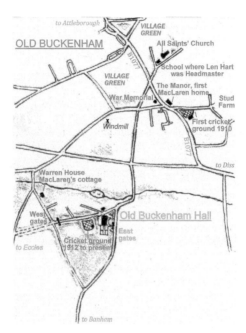

Old Buckenham locations.

Beginning to take over

It was in the winter of 1909-1910 that Lionel Robinson hired the ex-Kent professional Alec Hearne to oversee the creation of top-class cricket facilities on the Old Buckenham Hall estate. This involved laying out two entirely separate grounds over the next three years. The first pitch was on a field adjacent to Lionel's newly created stud farm, almost a mile from the hall. The new square was ready for use in July 1910, with the *Eastern Daily Press* stating that one of the Hearne family was to act as Robinson's groundsman and the name 'Hearne' did indeed appear in the most of the teams put out by the Old Buckenham village in early 1910. Although only one Hearne ever appeared in any given side, a variety of initials were offered in match scorecards: T, A, T.G., F, J.T., T.J. and T.T. Dodgy handwriting or even mischievousness may have led to the apparent profusion of Hearnes, when only one was actually employed. Reference to JW Hearne's history of the cricketing family Hearne, *Wheelwrights to Wickets*, (1996) indicates that many Hearnes with these initials did actually exist but also rules out the possibility that any significant member of the clan remained at Old Buckenham Hall over the 1910 season. Alas, the book is disappointing for historians of Norfolk cricket in that it makes absolutely no mention of the family's link with Lionel Robinson.

It was not until what was described as the 'cricket week' at Old Buckenham Hall in late July 1910 that the new ground was referred to in the *Eastern Daily Press*. Both before and after this, the village side was active but the

Lionel Robinson (second left) with his team in front of the pavilion at the first ground in 1910. MacLaren is far right with Jack Mason rear centre and Charles Robson standing second right.

press stated only that its home games took place at 'Old Buckenham'; presumably it was still playing on the existing wicket, which may have been on the village green, the largest in England. It was certainly the same group of players as those who represented the village in 1909, with the inclusion of the mystery Hearne. Robinson himself featured regularly and there were also a couple of effective contributions with the ball from a mysterious bowler, who was described as captain of the Stock Exchange Cricket Club and who was presumably one of Robinson's banking chums. Alas, we cannot even be sure of his name for he appears as both B.H.Conran and as B.H.Couran.[26]

'L Robinson's XI' made its reappearance with its debut being against Yarmouth Conservative Club on 26 July. This year it both played regularly and also fielded a significant number of cricketers with first-class and Test experience; notable players who played for Robinson in 1910 included Archie MacLaren,[27] Albert Lawton of Derbyshire, Albert Trott, Cyril Staples, Charles Robson of Hampshire and the Gaekwad of Baroda; several were regular visitors. There was little intermixing with the village club as, apart from Robinson himself, the shadowy B.H.Conran was virtually the only player to play for both village and hall sides. The *Eastern Daily Press* seems to have become confused on one occasion as a fixture dated

---

26   The *Eastern Daily Press* even fails to be consistent about this player's initials for, as well as 'B.H.', he also appears as "PH". For the purposes of brevity, he will be referred to as 'B.H. Conran' in all subsequent appearances in the text.

27   Given that MacLaren was soon to be appointed as Lionel's director of cricket, it is tempting to view his arrival in Old Buckenham at precisely the same time as the new cricket ground was opened as more than a coincidence. However, there is no evidence that Archie was anything other than just another visiting cricketer at this time.

Lionel Robinson hosts lunch at the first cricket ground, 1910,
Boyce the butler (right) in attendance.

to 10 September was assigned to Old Buckenham but the team included
six players with first-class experience (see Appendix) and should clearly
have been described as L Robinson's XI. The fact that victory was achieved
by a margin of 300 runs should have given the game away; Lionel, like
another wealthy businessman, Sir Julien Cahn, who was to follow him as
a bankroller of his own elevens, was keen to win and smiled fondly on
crushing victories. He would certainly have been pleased with the results
in 1910 as no fewer than 16 of the 20 games played by teams based in Old
Buckenham were won and only one was lost, against a strong Norfolk Club
and Ground (C & G) side. Unlike Cahn, he hated playing away from home;
only four of those 20 matches (including those featuring the village side)
involved travel to an away ground. Presumably Lionel was keen to play
the bountiful host whenever possible and didn't care to 'slum' it with the
locals when on the road, whilst his opponents would have been equally
keen to take advantage of his lavish hospitality.[28]

A dog's dinner
In 1911 Robinson continued to bankroll matches at Old Buckenham and
again his sides had a successful season; of the 18 games played for which
details survive, as many as 16 were played at home with no fewer than 12
being won and only four seeing defeat. Victory was gained in the three
most important games; in a rare trip to Norwich, Robinson's team crushed
the senior Norfolk side by seven wickets whilst the visiting Eton Ramblers

---

28   In passing one should note that this was Lionel's finest season with the
      bat. In 12 innings, nine of them completed, he amassed no fewer than 74
      runs, averaging 8.22. His top score was an unbeaten 27 against Quidenham
      Parsonage, an innings devalued by the fact that Old Buckenham had long
      since passed their opponents' score when Lionel went in to bat.

Queenie Robinson takes aim watched by her father Lionel, Old Buckenham, October 18, 1911. (Phillips-Getty Images)

A shoot at Old Buckenham , November 1, 1911 with Lionel Robinson (third right) and daughters Viola (far left) and Queenie. (Phillips-Getty Images)

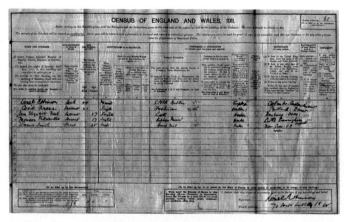

1911 Census - Lionel Robinson resident at his house in London's Mayfair.

*Lionel's London house at the height of his financial powers was
70 South Audley Street in Mayfair. (Tom Walshe)*

and 'A Norfolk XI' were defeated by ten runs and 199 runs respectively.

Unfortunately it is exceptionally hard to follow the cricketing doings of Robinson's elevens in this year. The impression given (probably correctly) is one of a cricketing fanatic with (much) more money than sense and an ego sufficiently large that none of his cronies were able to channel his spending into a rational programme. The reader is referred to the Appendix for a consideration of the total lack of logic in the nomenclature of the elevens put into the field by Robinson but an attempt to find any logic in the coming and going of players is equally doomed to failure. It seems over 80 cricketers turned out in 1911. One of the few patterns that one can observe is that the strengths of the various sides varied widely.

Fine cricketers such as Aubrey Faulkner, Gerry Weigall, Michael Falcon and Jack Mason 'popped in' for no more than a couple of matches each and most of the players appeared no more than three or four times; one of these infrequent visitors was Bernard Bosanquet, who was later to become something of a fixture on Lionel's estate. Among the more regular participants were Charles Robson and Archie MacLaren, who appeared in no fewer than 12 and seven matches respectively; but they had become more than semi-permanent guests at Old Buckenham by this point.[29] Other regulars included Albert Lawton, B.H.Conran, Lionel's employee William Groom (see below) and two figures even more shadowy than Conran: G.Clarke[30] and P.M.Hepworth. These last two were not 'hired guns' with first-class credentials nor were they local cricketers of note; they were not even villagers (few of whom got the chance to turn out any more).

Lionel himself played in only three games in 1911, being described in the press as a 'veteran'. A more apt word might have been a 'Jonah' for he played in two of his teams' four defeats.

William Groom – 'Squibs'

The name of W Groom already appears amongst those of the cricketers who turned out for the village team of Old Buckenham in 1908 and he was among the longest-lasting of the villagers; he survived to play no fewer than eight games for Robinson's teams in 1911 whilst his team-mates were being rapidly replaced by the 'foreigners' with their fancy caps. He even managed to be selected for a couple of matches in 1912 when the other villagers had disappeared from view altogether. When the village side was re-formed after the Great War, he was again one of its leading players. Although he had once been a chimney-sweep, he had taken up employment as Robinson's assistant groundsman, which probably gave him an advantage over his fellow villagers when it came to being selected to make up one of his master's elevens.

Although Philip Yaxley in *Looking Back at Norfolk Cricket* gives his name as Edward Groom, the *Eastern Daily Press* is clear that his given name was William; however, it was by his nickname, 'Squibs', that he gained a

---

29   Reference to *Kelly's Directory* for 1912, which references data collected in 1911, indicates that both Robson and MacLaren were actually resident on the estate during the 1911 season. The former was already a paid employee of Lionel's; he is described as 'head gamekeeper to Lionel G Robinson' and stated that he was residing at 'The Cottage'. Archie is referred to as living at 'The Manor', which had been vacated by Prince Freddy's sisters (the Princesses Bamba, Catherine and Sophia) in 1909 and which was close to the 'first' ground. Although there is no mention of paid employment for Archie in *Kelly's*, it is inconceivable that Archie had no input in the maintenance of the cricket facilities; however it is not clear when he officially assumed charge of cricketing operations for Lionel, although in its gossip column on 21 July 1912, the Perth Sunday Times reported: 'A.C. MacLaren, the English cricketer, has received the post of secretary to Lionel Robinson, who has decided to settle down at Old Buckenham Hall, Norfolk, and is a great cricket enthusiast. A lot of W.A. gold will go to pay Mr. MacLaren's salary.'

30   It is probable that 'G.Clarke' is, in fact, Garnet Leslie Clark, the son of Bill Clark, who was educated at Repton and who was sufficiently skilled to represent his school at cricket on more than one occasion. Cricketers of Garnet Clark's age certainly appear in pictures of Robinson's sides at this time.

Lionel Robinson plays international host to South African, Australian and home players in 1912. (Philip Yaxley)

Sid Pegler, 19 first-class wickets in four games for Lionel. (Roger Mann)

Bernard Bosanquet, a regular at Old Buckenham and Lionel's favourite captain. (Roger Mann)

The redoubtable Squibs (William Groom), countryman and cricketer.
(Ian MacLaren's album, courtesy of Michael Down)

local fame. By 1920 the *Eastern Daily Press* no longer referred to him in match scorecards by his real name but simply as 'Squibs' (having passed through an intermediate phase of referring to him as 'W.Squibs'). Yaxley describes 'Squibs' as 'somewhat retarded' but 'a great-hearted little chap and a fine enthusiastic cricketer' and he was, according to local author Michael Home, regarded as being unreliable with the bat but was highly valued for his willingness to 'bowl all day and never tire and lose heart'. Home was writing of pre-War days however and, after the War, 'Squibs' had to move with the times; the arrival in Old Buckenham of Len Hart, who also liked to bowl all day and was good enough to do so (see chapter four), meant that Groom had to reinvent himself as a batsman. That he did so successfully was shown in the averages published in the *Eastern Daily Press*. In 1920 (when he claimed only 22 wickets) he finished fourth in the batting list and was invited to bat for the South Norfolk League representative side; whilst in 1923, a year in which he does not seem to have bowled at all for Old Buckenham, he was second only to Hart. In 1924 'Squibs' had the finest day of his career by scoring 102 not out (of the team's total of 174) for Old Buckenham against Quidenham District; in those days individual centuries in village cricket were as rare as hens' teeth and he must have been either a considerably better bat than Michael Home believed or had an extraordinarily lucky day at the wicket. 'Squibs' was still a capable enough cricketer to be playing in games appropriate to players well above his social status as late as 1927.

Home, whilst confessing an ignorance of 'Squibs'' real name, hints that Groom might not have been quite as 'retarded' as posterity seems to have recorded. He appears to have been a keen bird-watcher and Home draws attention to his habit of writing letters to the *Eastern Daily Press* regarding matters ornithological. These were written both under the name of W Groom and as 'Squibs' and, although they were not works of great literary merit, they were clearly not the work of an imbecile. One will be given in full, to give some idea of the level of erudition which was typical for 'Squibs':

> *'The account of a robin's nest in an old jam jar is interesting. Last year the head gardener at Old Buckenham showed me a wagtail's nest in a well-head garden[?] vase between three marguerite daisies. The gardeners were watering frequently, but it made no difference as she hatched off her young ones. A robin also built its nest in an old glass bottle which lay upon a bank with its neck knocked off in some nettles – Yours truly, W Groom.'*

A shrewd view might be that, whilst 'Squibs' might not have been the sharpest pencil in the box, he actively played on his image as 'lovable idiot' to secure a regular game of cricket and a free feed (it is not clear which he appreciated most, just that he was very keen on both). Alas, in the end Home reports that 'his wits gave way and he died at quite an early age in an asylum', being sorely missed in local cricketing circles.

Chapter Three:

Putting Old Buckenham on the cricketing map – Archie MacLaren starts to earn his beer money

Lionel hires Archie

Whenever Archie MacLaren actually moved his family to the estate at Old Buckenham, Lionel had formally appointed him as his 'private secretary', effectively manager of cricket, by the start of the 1912 season. Some sources, such as Jeremy Malies, state that he was also put in charge of Robinson's stud farm, but this seems to be unlikely; Lionel and his partner William Clark had been successfully involved in the breeding of horses for many years (as will be described below) and knew far more about racing than Archie. Malies states that MacLaren hired a few experienced grooms and, pretending to know what he was doing, hoped for the best but few, if any, details of his involvement with the equestrian operation survive; he was, by nature, fond of 'slow horses' and Malies reports that a later attempt to run a stud farm was 'disastrous'. However it was achieved, Archie's appointment to manage the cricket turned out to be an inspired choice. Robinson had top-quality facilities, large amounts of money to spend and (probably) an awareness that he needed a knowledgeable and influential figure to run his cricket operations efficiently. A suitable candidate could not, obviously, be a professional, nor would Lionel feel able to defer to a 'junior' amateur; the successful applicant would need to be a gentleman of considerable standing in the world of cricket[31] and, furthermore, one nearing the end of his first-class career; for it would be very difficult to continue playing if most of his time was spent in the middle of nowhere. In hindsight, Archie MacLaren was the obvious choice. Not only was he, as ever, dodging the bailiffs and desperate for regular employment to pay for his regular intake of falling-down water, he also had suitable Antipodean credentials. Michael Down and Colin Riley both

---

31 Evelyn Metcalfe recounts a tale of some bad behaviour by Lionel which exemplified the need for a captain with both authority and self-confidence who could stand up to his employer. Metcalfe found himself captaining a team including Aubrey Faulkner who was, at that time, at the peak of his power as a bowler of leg-breaks and googlies and far too skilful for the visiting side. Inevitably, Metcalfe found himself enforcing the follow-on but, taking pity on his hapless opponents, he declined to put Faulkner on to bowl. Unsurprisingly, wickets fell more slowly and Lionel began to fear that an outright victory would elude his team. He began to rage on the boundary, shouting for Faulkner to be put on. When the sky filled with black clouds he became even more animated and his skipper finally yielded; Faulkner was given the ball just in time to finish off the innings before a torrential thunderstorm. In his account in *The Cricketer*, Metcalfe states that it was the fear that he might never be invited to Old Buckenham again that finally induced him to use Faulkner - it is not entirely clear that he was joking ...

Lionel Robinson, very much the country squire, relaxing in the grounds of Old Buckenham Hall. (Ian MacLaren album, courtesy of Michael Down)

point out that that Robinson would almost certainly have known Archie's in-laws in Melbourne in the 1890s where Archie had married Maud Power, daughter of Robert Power, a wealthy landowner and businessman and a fellow member of the Melbourne Cricket Club and Victoria Racing Club.

Lionel duly installed Archie, Maud and their two children in a property in the village known as 'The Manor', from where they moved to 'The Warren' (now 'Warren House') by 1916.

There are three aspects of MacLaren's cricket that require a few words of consideration: his status as a player, his competence as a manager of men and his ability to organise an operation such as that required by Robinson. As a player, MacLaren more than fitted the bill. He was one of the greatest batsmen of cricket's 'Golden Age'. Clem Hill stated that he was the finest batsman ever to visit Australia and two innings (of 109 and 50 not out) played at a Sydney Test in 1897-8 produced the following piece of purple prose: 'the sheer magnificence of his batsmanship ... caused Sydney cricketers to talk about it, dream about it all, over again, for years.' On a tricky wicket at the Lord's Test of 1905 he played an innings of 79 that C.B.Fry described as: 'Regal and Incredible.' Though he preferred to play off the front foot, he was more than competent with the hook shot and is well known as the first batsman to hit a quadruple century in first-class cricket; playing against Somerset at Taunton in 1895 he amassed 424 at a rate of 50 runs an hour, hitting one six and 62 fours. He was one of the great stylists of the 'Golden Age', as has been expertly documented by Michael Down in his biography, *Archie*. He was almost as noted a fielder as he was a batsman, being a stylish square-leg and a superb first-slip, noted for his powers of anticipation and his ability to use either hand. Importantly, although well aware that he was past his prime for cricket at the highest level, he was still able to contribute significantly as a batsman to the teams that he captained for Robinson. Perhaps trading on his reputation as a Test cricketer, he was also able to put himself on to bowl for Robinson's sides on many occasions with much more success than a first-class bowling average of 267.00 would suggest. At least once, in 1913, he even took on the role of wicketkeeper.

Archie's captaincy famously received rave reviews from Neville Cardus but rather more dispassionate observers have pointed out that a record in Ashes Tests of four wins and 11 losses in 22 games is not one would expect of a truly great skipper and many revisionist historians have levelled accusations of poor man-management against him. Evidence of an unhelpful streak of pessimism has been cited; for example, when shown the side chosen for the Old Trafford Test of 1902 he was quoted as saying: 'My God, Jacker [Sir Stanley Jackson], look what they've sent me. Do they think I am playing the blind asylum?' Furthermore, although he could be a shrewd judge of the game, he also had 'moments of madness' when his grasps of selection and tactics seemed far from sure. Archie has been portrayed as possessing an experienced cricket brain that was capable of instinctive brilliance, but being cursed with a capricious streak which could make him his own worst enemy. Critical spectators at home Tests were known to find that his placing of the field and his changing of the bowling were sometimes 'eccentric and misguided'. To be fair to Archie, Michael Down thinks that the critics have been far too harsh, blaming selectorial errors attributed to his subject on the selectors who, the author claims, over-ruled their captain. He also states that 'there has always been unanimous agreement that [Archie] had no peer when it came to tactical matters', with the one exception that he was loathe to take off a successful, but tiring, bowler in favour of a fresh change bowler. That exception could prove costly; on the Ashes Tour of 1901-2 the over-bowling of Sydney Barnes undoubtedly contributed to his breakdown while refusal to remove 'Daddy' Carr from the attack during the Oval Test in 1909 is frequently cited as an archetypal piece of misjudgement.

However, Archie certainly had the bearings of a Test skipper, it being said that he was: 'one of the most commanding cricketers ... whether doing well or not so well', that: 'from his position at first slip...his gesture was regal' and that he had 'lofty self-assurance ... [and an] imperious attitude'. He could, though, show a common touch; Malies reveals that: 'At a time when Lord Harris and Lord Hawke were treating professionals as though they had communicable diseases, nothing gave Archie more pleasure than skipping down the pavilion steps with his arm round Johnny Tyldesley.'

What is undeniably to his credit is that he discovered Sydney Barnes, arguably the finest bowler that the Test game has ever seen, plucking him from almost complete obscurity to go on an Ashes tour. Unfortunately though, he seems to have got things wrong rather too often. Malies states, somewhat ambivalently: 'The subject is a farrago, an extraordinary mass

Lionel Robinson's first cricket ground at Old Buckenham, now a paddock at the stud farm with the thatched pavilion converted to a dwelling. (Ron Brewer)

of contradictions and a character at once ambiguous, driven and revealing of his time. At times Archie could be warm, insensitive, charming and arrogant. He could combine ... the most staggering misjudgements and the most piercing insights.' Others were even less kind. George Lyttleton said: 'It is disillusioning to realise that Majestic MacLaren was an extremely stupid, prejudiced and pig-headed man' and John Arlott more or less finished him off with: 'It was MacLaren's tragedy that all his virtues bred their own faults. He was strong but inflexible, intelligent but intolerant: single-minded but humourless; impressive on the field but often disappointingly petty off it.' One sign of his pettiness was that, as Mailes wrote, when the MCC chose 'Plum' Warner to captain the 1903-4 Ashes tour, 'he [MacLaren] refused point-blank to tour under Warner and vented his frustrations by spattering abuse in some graceless articles ...' in the *Daily Chronicle*.

Where Archie did score most highly was that he had a proven record in managing top-class cricket and moving in all the right circles; he had made three Ashes tours, having been in charge of the last two, and he knew everyone who was anyone in the upper echelons of English cricket. This enabled him both to persuade many first-class players to turn out for Lionel's teams[32] ensuring that competitive and well-balanced elevens were put into the field in a logical programme of fixtures and also to persuade the authorities to confer first-class status on the most prestigious matches at Old Buckenham. Whilst his colonial background would have carried weight in persuading Australians to visit Norfolk, both as individuals and in touring sides, it is harder to imagine that the brash, brusque

---

32   Given Archie's imperious manner and senior status, it is easy to imagine that many of the younger players that he 'invited' to Old Buckenham, who were on the periphery of the first-class game, might have found that they had little choice but to agree to make the trip to Norfolk.

Robinson (for who the term 'new money' could have been invented) would have acquired anything like the recognition that he did without such an acceptable and capable 'front man' as MacLaren.[33]

As will become clear, Archie's time as Robinson's manager of cricket was extremely successful – even, perhaps, the most successful phase of his lengthy cricket career, leading directly as it did to his famous victory over the seemingly invincible Australian tourists of 1921 at Eastbourne with a scratch side of his own choosing (see chapter six). As stated above, he was still able to bat with success and with much of his old style and the press was uniformly complimentary about his captaincy and leadership skills. Whether the 'old dog' had learnt 'new tricks' and mellowed as a skipper or whether the press just took a more lenient view of his captaincy in his dotage is unclear.

The puzzle of Lionel's forgotten ground

Before discussing the fortunes of Robinson's teams under the direction of Archie, the matter of Lionel's two separate cricket grounds must be dealt with. Lionel appears to have been a perfectionist and, just as he was not satisfied with his first attempt to construct a new hall, he also decided to lay down a second cricket pitch. This was made in a clearing in the woods adjacent to the hall in readiness for the start of the 1912 season, and is the pitch still in use today. The *Eastern Daily Press* refers to the new ground but does not state explicitly that it was a second pitch and, as a result, the existence of the first ground has been more or less forgotten. One elderly resident of Old Buckenham still remembers that her father had spoken of cricket being played on an area which is now a paddock in the stud farm; all that remains of this is the pavilion, which has been converted to a thatched bungalow. This has a roof and an overall size and shape that are compatible with those of the building which is assumed to be the pavilion shown in pictures that date to matches played on Lionel's 'first ground' in 1910. The pavilion constructed for the second cricket ground is still in existence, but elsewhere (see chapter seven) and is markedly different in structure from that from the first ground; it is clearly not the building seen in the 'early' photographs and confirms that Lionel had two altogether different playing areas constructed.

From the map of the estate showing the location of Lionel's two grounds, it can be seen that the 'second ground' is almost within a six-hit of the hall

---

33   There was nothing in MacLaren's personal life to suggest that he would make a capable manager of anything. Although he had been educated at Elstree and Harrow, his family were not 'old money'; nor were they even 'new money', but genuinely 'no money' as his father, James MacLaren, had been a cotton merchant who had virtually bankrupted himself in educating his seven sons. Archie exacerbated his own financial problems by his inability to manage what money he did possess and his tendency to get involved in pea-brained schemes which always failed to yield any profits. Even the regular allowance that came with his marriage to Maud Power in 1898 failed to prevent him from being convicted for the non-payment of rates in 1908. At various times before taking Robinson's shilling he worked in the Manchester & Liverpool Bank, taught at a prep school, dabbled in journalism (notably for the *Daily Chronicle*) and served as secretary to Ranjitsinhji in India between 1905 and 1908. Unfortunately, Ranji had no more clue about ordering his finances than did Archie and was permanently living on 'tick'.

which would have made the catering arrangements for the lavish lunches, for which Lionel was famous, much easier to organise. According to the *Eastern Daily Press,* it seems that Alec Hearne was called in for the second time in two years and set to build from scratch once again. A somewhat unhelpful account of proceedings is given in an article by Evelyn Metcalfe in *The Cricketer* in which the author claims the credit, not just for the idea of creating 'a good cricket ground in the Park' in the first place, but also for overseeing the whole process, claiming that his friend Robinson gave him *carte blanche* to organise proceedings. He makes no reference to the 'first' ground. This story is far from corroborated by Barry Wilson, writing in the *Sunday Times* many years later, who credits the lord of the manor with being well-informed on the matter of the construction of a satisfactory wicket and very much in charge of operations. Wilson states that Robinson, who had watched much cricket both at Melbourne and around England, was no fan of slow English wickets and wanted his own wicket to be hard and fast. There was a lagoon on his estate which he had dredged to obtain fine clay which would provide the foundation for the square and he had the soil stabilised with chicken netting. Although he was nothing more than an enthusiastic amateur, Robinson was successful in creating a fast wicket and further improved the playing surface after the Great War by importing soil from his native Australia. Even at the much later date when Wilson was writing (1977), the part of the Old Buckenham square which had been laid by Robinson that was still in use (known as the 'Australian end') remained quicker than the newer part of the square.[34] Wilson, like Metcalfe, completely ignores both the existence of the 'first' ground and the presence of MacLaren, who would surely have 'stuck his oar in' as an interested party.

1912: Archie's debut as cricket manager

Archie's first season as Lionel Robinson's cricket manager must be judged a highly successful one. He arranged a well-balanced programme of 12 matches (down from the rather chaotic 18 played in the previous year), all of which were played at home (presumably on the 'second' pitch) and no fewer than nine finished in victory for Lionel's sides. The only setback was in the very first match of the season, when a virtually full-strength Norfolk county side defeated a not particularly strong Robinson's XI by eight wickets. The home batting, which contained three Australians, failed twice against the county's professional bowlers; both Harold Watson and Ted Gibson took six-wicket hauls as Robinson's side were dismissed for 163 and 142. Only Philip Slater, who played one first-class game for Surrey, resisted for long as he made 64 at his first attempt. Norfolk's first

---

34   The puzzle is made even more complex by the existence of a letter from Donald Sewell, who was bought up at Old Buckenham Hall, played cricket for the village during the 1940s and 1950s and who later became headmaster of the Old Buckenham Hall School when it had moved to Brettenham Park (see chapter seven). Sewell states categorically that the 'fact' that turf was imported from Australia is a myth and that, although high-quality marl was brought into Norfolk, it was merely from Nottinghamshire. This version of events is backed up by a contemporary report in the Australian press, which also refers to the addition of soil from Devon to the square. However, the *Eastern Daily Press*, in a 1921 article, talks of a 'special mixture... imported from "down under" where the world's best wickets are to be found'.

Archie and Maud MacLaren at the races.
(Ian MacLaren album, courtesy of Michael Down)

Archie MacLaren at home in Old Buckenham.
(Ian MacLaren album, courtesy of Michael Down)

innings went little better but Geoffrey Stevens made an unbeaten 66 to see the county home with plenty to spare. It is the commentary on this game in the local press that dates the laying out of this 'new' ground under the supervision of Alec Hearne; the *Eastern Evening News* explicitly stated that 'Mr Robinson opened his charming new ground'. Several hundred spectators attended, despite chilly weather – not for the last time was Robinson's enjoyment of an important match marred by inclement conditions.

A routine victory over CEYMS (Church of England Young Men's Society) followed, with five-wicket hauls being taken by Michael Falcon and Reggie Schwarz and half-centuries for Eric Fulcher and Archie (the latter batting in 'his own masterly style'). The next two matches were also relatively low-key victories, over the 5th Battalion of the Rifle Brigade, and Stow and District. The latter were beaten by an innings; after the eccentric Gerry Weigall had made an unbeaten 68, Archie showed his versatility by taking seven for 49 to ensure that Old Buckenham Hall would not have to bat again. The fifth match was a high-scoring draw against Carrow; an unbeaten 107 from 'Old George' Pilch saw the visitors declare at 287 for five and, after Old Buckenham Hall lost three early wickets, Geoffrey Stevens and Archie played out time, scoring 119 not out and 75 not out respectively as Hall closed on 210 for three.

The first match of the Old Buckenham Hall Week featured a home eleven that had a very South African feel about it, with Frank Mitchell, Reggie Schwarz, Sid Pegler and Harold Baumgartner (all of whom had, or would, play Test cricket) being available to play for Robinson's team against the Oxford University Authentics. Pegler took seven for 57 with his leg-breaks in the first innings whilst Baumgartner claimed five for 69 with his slow left arm in the second as the Authentics were shot out for just 156 and 158. In response, Hall batted steadily to reach 258 in their first innings (Archie top-scoring with 67) and got home with seven wickets to spare, in spite of Pegler 'bagging a pair'.

The following match is the subject of a story, published in *The Cricketer* by Evelyn Metcalfe, which purports to give evidence of Lionel's unconventional approach to friendly cricket. Metcalfe stated that he was responsible for taking an MCC side to Old Buckenham and, as Robinson had 12 players on hand, he had to co-opt Schwarz at the last minute. Metcalfe stated that the first day was completely lost to rain and play could not start until 1pm on the second day. By this stage the pitch was sodden and useless for bowling; furthermore the ball quickly assumed the consistency of a 'pudding' so that batting was relatively trouble-free. The opening pair, two (unidentified) members of the Australian touring side batted until 6pm, when stumps were pulled with the score over 300 runs and no wickets down. Given that batsmen of the calibre of Geoffrey Foster, Bernard Bosanquet and Archie MacLaren were left sitting in the pavilion, Metcalfe described the innings as a 'huge farce'; in contrast Lionel 'roared with laughter and was highly pleased'. Metcalfe went on to state that he suggested to his host that he ought to have declared upon reaching 200 and tried to bowl out the MCC but that Robinson was content that he had given the visitors 'a real good leather hunting'. Unfortunately this tale appears to have had almost no basis in truth; even Sir Neville Cardus at his most inventive would have blanched at such an outrageous tissue of falsehoods. The match, which took place on 1 and 2 July, was a standard eleven-a-side affair and, although it did indeed finish with the strange-looking score, Robinson's XI only managed to accumulate 262 before the game terminated.[35] Furthermore, the two Australian openers, W.L. Jack (who scored 93) and Rupert Minnett (who reached 156), were relatively obscure and not members of the touring side at all. More importantly, it was the second day that was rained off rather than the first; Robinson's team were thus guilty of nothing more than building a sizeable first-innings score whilst conditions were favourable. No-one could have known that the lack of further play would render the whole innings futile. Metcalfe stands exposed as a fraud – but the very fact that he could even consider telling such an outrageous story against Lionel Robinson suggests that there was 'no smoke without fire' and that his readers would be expecting tales of his host to feature some eccentric 'colonial' behaviour[36]

Prolonged rain delayed the start of the third and final match of the Old Buckenham Hall Week until 2pm on the first day, and the wicket played as badly as might have been expected until the close of play. The Incogniti were tumbled out for 88, largely due to Schwarz who took six for 16 off 15.1 overs with his googlies but Hall could do little better, losing nine wickets for 96 when the absence of the mysterious 'H.A.Barmey' caused the innings to be closed. Conran made his mark by taking three for seven against rather than for Lionel's eleven. Use of the roller meant that the

Archie MacLaren with son Ian wildfowling on The Warren, Old Buckenham.
(Ian MacLaren album, courtesy of Michael Down)

---

35   It would be of interest to know if there has ever been a match, at any level, in which no wicket fell and more than 262 runs were scored.

36   Not for the only time, Metcalfe enjoyed telling a tale so much that this appeared twice in *The Cricketer*.

wicket was more batsman-friendly on the second day but the Incogniti could still do no better than score 196, with Schwarz bringing his bag of wickets for the match to ten. This could still have proved a difficult target but the Harlequin, Wilfrid Lord, with an unbeaten 61 and the mysterious Barmey (who was, according to the *Eastern Daily Press*, an English Test player who wished to remain anonymous for reasons which were not made clear) with a rapid 57, hit in just half an hour, meant that Hall took a mere 89 minutes to knock off the runs. Barmey's innings contained nine fours and he took 18 runs off one over from Gerald Campbell before having his wicket rearranged by Conran.

A straightforward win by nine wickets (over two innings) over King's Lynn was followed by a match against the Harrow Blues, which contained the performance that stood out as the most meritorious seen in any of the games played at Old Buckenham Hall during Lionel's ownership. Reginald Popham and Rupert Minnett put on no less than 463 runs for Hall's second wicket and, when the partnership was broken, it was due to a run out. Popham was dismissed for 226 whilst Minnett had accumulated an unbeaten 291 (his second giant score at Old Buckenham that season) when Archie called a halt to the slaughter at 563 for three. Unsurprisingly the Blues put up little resistance, making just 80 and 55 – in their second innings no fewer than 24 of the runs scored were extras and no batsman reached double figures. Harold Baumgartner took seven wickets in their first innings whilst Frank Tuff bagged seven of his own in their second knock.

Touring Elevens In Norfolk

There was now a hiatus in the cricket at Old Buckenham for a couple of weeks while Lionel busied himself in helping to organise the visit of the Australian tourists to Norwich (as referred to in the Introduction). Reports in the *Eastern Daily Press* of 3,000 seats being made available at prices of two shillings, 2s 6d and 5s (the latter guaranteeing a front row seat) with motors and bicycles incurring fees of 2s 6d and 3d respectively contrast all too starkly with the arrangements at Old Buckenham Hall, where free entry was available for all; however Lionel was very much richer than the county club. Unfortunately, this game was dogged by bad weather, like so many others in the wet summer of 1912. Norfolk secretary Charles Prior reached the ground early on what should have been the first day of the match, took one look at the conditions and telephoned Lionel to cancel the catering arrangements for lunch and to alert the amateur players staying at the Hall that they would not be required to play that day. At around 11am, the skipper of the England XI, Bernard Bosanquet, made use of his host Lionel's phone to contact the Australian captain, Sid Gregory, who was staying at the Maid's Head Hotel in Norwich, so that play could be officially called off for the day. The groundsman likened the appearance of the ground to Breydon Water, a rather bleak expanse of water near Great Yarmouth, and, to add to the desolation, the high wind had blown over many tents and marquees which were floating about forlornly. The Australians were not expecting there to be much play on the following day, but Lakenham was a quick-drying ground and, once a fresh wicket had been cut and rolled, play could have started by midday. Unfortunately the storm had disrupted communications with Old Buckenham; neither telephone nor telegram links were functioning and a motorcycle had to be sent to summon the home team while the tourists were left twiddling their thumbs. Play started after lunch before a few hundred spectators. There was bright sunshine for a while but then heavy rain returned at 4pm to terminate play for the day. The third day saw around five hours' play but, despite 25 wickets falling for just 290 runs, a result never looked on the cards. There was, at least, a decent crowd of 2,000 or so spectators on the last day but the *Eastern Daily Press* reported that 'the expenses of the match were heavy, and the cricket loving public owe a debt of gratitude to the gentlemen who arranged and guaranteed the match'. As stated in the Introduction, Lionel was undoubtedly one of these 'gentlemen'. With the infrastructure of Norfolk having been placed under extreme pressure by the torrents of rain, the Australian tourists had difficulty making their way out of the county and on to Canterbury for their next game; they had to be driven by car to Wymondham before they were able to catch a train.

Returning to his favourite pastime of beating up local cricket clubs, Lionel enjoyed another low-key, single-innings win over Dereham. Kenneth Hutchings scored 59 and took four wickets but the match was only notable for Robinson himself making his second appearance of the year and his only visit to the crease. Batting at number ten, he scored only a single out of a total of 147 and, as in his previous appearance against Carrow, neither took a wicket or held a catch.

The season culminated with the visit of the South Africans to Old Buckenham for a game which was deemed to have been of first-class status. Before describing this match it is worth considering the opinions of the correspondents of the national newspapers on Lionel's wicket. The *Guardian* stated that the pitch was in 'capital condition, but rather fast, and batsmen found the pace too much for them'. The *Daily Telegraph* declared that Old Buckenham Hall was a 'splendid cricket ground ... many batsmen being troubled by the fast pace of the pitch'. The *Times* made it unanimous when it referred to the pitch on the first day: 'after the slow grounds on which they have had to play lately the batsmen found the rather fast turf too much for them'. That all three papers should go out of their way to comment on the quick pace of the wicket when none gave the match extensive coverage, is surely an indication that the wicket was genuinely pacy and that, whoever was involved in its creation and whenever the work was carried out, it was already possessed of the characteristics desired by Lionel Robinson in time for its first appearance in a first-class match. [37]

No doubt the speed of the Old Buckenham wicket would have been a surprise to the touring South Africans, but to what extent the home team would have been forewarned is not entirely clear. Archie had asked

---

37   A modern writer, Patrick Ferriday, suggests that the strip may even have been a little too fast, stating that the wicket was 'hard and fast enough to shock almost everyone into submission'.

*Warren House at Old Buckenham, the MacLaren family home
for several years until 1921.
(Ian MacLaren album, courtesy of Michael Down)*

Bosanquet, who had not played at Old Buckenham earlier in the year, and thus had no experience of the turf, to skipper Lionel's side and, when he won the toss, he naturally chose to bat first. This proved to be a disastrous move as the first five wickets fell for just 30 runs, the captain himself failing to trouble the scorers. At this point Alfred Evans was joined by Michael Falcon and they added a rapid 71 runs, ending with 48 and 29 respectively. Apart from a youngish 'Patsy' Hendren, who scored 27 batting at nine, no one else reached double figures as Robinson's side limped to a total of 153, presumably blaming their poor showing in the wicket. Sid Pegler took six for 45, the first of many meritorious performances at Old Buckenham Hall. When the South Africans went in to bat, their innings followed a similar course. The first five wickets put on a mere 16 and only some resistance from the lower middle order enabled the tourists to reach 151, a deficit of just two runs. The most effective bowler was Falcon, who finished with six for 47, having caused the early collapse by taking five of the first six wickets. Over his career, Falcon fell just short of the highest pace but, in 1912, he was at his fastest and, given the helpful nature of the wicket, is it easy to imagine that the South Africans would have found his pace a little hard to handle, especially as he was able to make good use of a biting wind. In contrast, it was reported that Harry Dean was unable to spin the ball owing to the extreme cold; he then completed a miserable match by straining a ligament after bowling just five overs and took no further part.

Robinson's batsmen made a much better fist of their second innings. Hendren, promoted to number three, made 80 in just 75 minutes while opener Frank Tarrant fell just one short of a half century. The score had reached 254 for seven when heavy rain caused play to be abandoned for the rest of the second day and the innings closed at 255 early the next morning, with Pegler returning figures of five for 75 for a match haul of

11 for 120. The South Africans thus had virtually a whole day in which to score 258 for victory. Unfortunately for them, the rain that had curtailed the second day's play was followed by bright sunshine and the result was that the wicket turned into an old-fashioned 'sticky dog' on which they had no chance against the slowish left arm spin of Tarrant and the pacier Harry Simms. Each took five wickets, with Tarrant's figures of 14-10-8-5 being particularly impressive. The tourists could only manage 66, with only Herbie Taylor and Gordon White making double figures. The tourists were not rated a particularly strong team but the margin of defeat, a crushing 191 runs, gave an unfairly poor impression of their calibre to the crowd of 'several hundred' who turned up to watch play on the third day.[38] It has been suggested that the tourists did not take this match entirely seriously but their misfortune would not have troubled Lionel Robinson one bit; he would have been extremely happy with a massive win over tourists who had Test status.

Intriguingly, a note appeared in the *Eastern Daily Press* in September 1912: 'We are informed by Mr Lionel Robinson that there is no truth in the report published in Melbourne that he is taking out an English cricket team to Australia.' This sentence is something of a puzzle; Robinson was reluctant for his teams to play even a few miles from Old Buckenham and they never ventured beyond the county boundaries of Norfolk. There is no hint anywhere else that the one-time globetrotter, having settled down, showed any desire whatsoever to export 'his' cricket. The existence of a possible unofficial tour was also reported in the Australian press, which suggested that either Robinson or Sir Abe Bailey, a keen financier of cricket from South Africa, was behind the proposed venture but no more was heard of this shadowy proposition.

Racing Success and the Stud Farm
Lionel started investing in horse-racing in England in 1898 and he and Bill Clark were among the first owners to transport high-quality horses from England to Australia. They enjoyed many victories in important races, including one of the world's most prestigious events, the Melbourne Cup, which they took with the aptly named four-year-old, The Victory, in 1902.[39] More big wins in Australia came courtesy of Rienzi (South Australian Derby, 1902), King Offa (Caulfield Cup), St Spasa (the Metropolitan Stakes), Eudoros and Flash of Steel (both winners of the Caulfield Futurity Stakes) and Lucknow (winner of both the Caulfield Cup and the Caulfield Futurity Stakes). An article in *The Australian* lauded the ability of Bill Clark, both as a tipster worth following and as the owner of a profitable string of horses.[40]

---

38   Admission to Robinson's ground was, as usual, free, even though the match had been granted first-class status.
39   The Melbourne Cup was the richest of all the Australian races and winning it was a boyhood ambition for Lionel but neither he nor Clark travelled from England to be present at the triumph of The Victory; they did, however, make themselves popular by organising for £200 of their winnings to be donated to various Australian charities.
40   Their racing colours were dark blue, rose and lavender.

Robinson and Clark also enjoyed huge racing success in England; although competition was fiercer and victories less frequent before the Great War, Lionel's brother, W.S, states that the pair 'were amongst the most successful owners and their winnings were substantial'. Their horses were initially trained by Sam Darling at Beckhampton but were moved to Newmarket in 1904 and entrusted to J.E. Brewer, another Australian. When the stud at Old Buckenham was constructed, William Clark was listed as a co-owner. Many good winners were produced by the stud; perhaps the best was Prince Galahad, who was considered a potential winner of a classic. Having won the 1919 Dewhurst Stakes, the top race for two-year-olds, he was a strong fancy for the following year's 2,000 Guineas before he 'went wrong'. He had beaten Tetratema, the horse that went on to win the Guineas, in a trial run on level terms. Another profitable horse was Stefan the Great, which was co-owned with a Joseph E Widner; however, he was not sired until 1916 and Lionel was unable to enjoy the success at stud which led to him being champion broodmare sire in 1939. Around 15 mares of the 'best type' were kept at Old Buckenham Hall. To give some idea of the money involved in running a successful stud, the owners paid £10,000 for the mare Pamfleta and her filly foal by The Tetrarch, a famous stallion who fathered many winning horses and who was Champion Sire in 1919. They later sold the foal, Idumea, for 5100 guineas, also netting 6000 guineas for Reine Des Peches and 5000 guineas for Petrea. Whilst prize money was relatively small in those days, significant numbers of beer-tokens could be made through betting and Lionel and Clark were, unsurprisingly, major gamblers. To give one example, they entered their horse Demure for the Cesarewitch in 1907, and by placing bets for themselves and for their friends back in Australia, they forced its odds to be cut from 100-1 down to 5-2 in the ante-post betting. Luckily for all concerned (except the bookies), Demure pulled off a narrow win.

In later years, Robinson contributed articles to *The Times* on both racing and breeding matters and, according to the *Eastern Evening News* commenting on his demise, although he was a 'generous patron of cricket ... his chief hobby [was] the conduct of a good breeding stud'. The idea that Lionel was a man of the turf first and a cricket enthusiast second was also proposed by his brother, W.S., who stated that 'Old Buckenham was ... a famous cricketing centre ... [but] was even better known for the racehorses bred on its two thousand acres'. It is entirely possible that it was the interest of Robinson and Clark in horse racing that induced the former to buy the estate at Old Buckenham, for it was handily placed to do business with the stud and training facilities at nearby Newmarket. As Clark seemed to have been little interested in cricket, Robinson had to 'fly solo' when he turned to that game and, as he had already spent so much rebuilding the Hall at Old Buckenham, he was committed to using that as a base, even though it was remote from the centres of high quality cricket.[41]

---

41   Michael Robinson concurs with the viewpoint that horse breeding rather than cricket was the most important activity that took place at Old Buckenham and it was this that led to Lionel's chosen location. See www.bloodlines.net/ TB/Bios2/TheTetrarch.htm

Robinson And Hockey

Whilst Robinson's interest in cricket and horse racing are well-known, his support for field hockey has all but been forgotten. One of the few surviving pieces of evidence is the following paragraph, from the *Norfolk Chronicle* of 6 January 1912, headlined:

FAMOUS CRICKETER'S LEG BROKEN: *While playing for Mr Lionel Robinson's eleven against the Norwich Wanderers, at Old Buckenham on Monday, G.A. Faulkner, the former* [sic] *South African cricketer, fell and fractured his leg. The accident occurred during a mix-up round goal. At the time the score was 1-1, but the regrettable occurrence took all interest out of the game, which was won by the Norwich team by 6 goals to 1... RO Schwarz, the South African 'googley' bowler, obtained the goal for Mr Robinson's team which also included such well-known cricketers as BJT Bosanquet and AE Lawton.*

This passage indicates that the Old Buckenham team was packed with Robinson's favourite cricketers and therefore suggests that 'his' players continued to enjoy his hospitality during the close season. Alas, it is unclear whether Lionel put out hockey[42] elevens at other times; local historian, Roger Wilson, has failed to uncover any evidence of further activity and Tom Walshe has suggested that this may have been a 'scratch' side raised from guests who were already present at Old Buckenham, enjoying their host's excellent shooting facilities.[43]

Mare and foal at Old Buckenham Stud around 1919.
(Ian MacLaren album, courtesy of Michael Down)

---

42 Australian sources insist that Faulkner injured himself playing association football rather than hockey, and state that Archie MacLaren was refereeing the game.

43 As well as facilities for cricket, shooting and hockey, Lionel also had tennis courts, billiard rooms and card rooms available for his guests, for whom nothing was too good.

Chapter Four:
Further Successes At Old Buckenham

1913: not Bosanquet again?

Having found a winning formula in managing Lionel Robinson's cricket in 1912, Archie MacLaren made the reasonable assumption that a similar programme of matches in 1913 would also please his employer – providing that the victories continued. Hence he organised a fixture list of eleven matches (one of which was scratched in mid-season so, eventually, only ten matches took place; two less than the previous year), all but one of which were due to be played at Old Buckenham Hall. The players he persuaded to travel to Norfolk performed so well that seven matches resulted in the comfortable or overwhelming victories that Robinson so coveted and victory in another was only denied by rain. The two defeats were both at the hands of elevens raised by Bernard Bosanquet. The season opened with the first loss, by the narrow margin of five runs. Both sides were packed with players who had played first-class cricket, and four regulars had experience of playing Test cricket: Bosanquet, MacLaren, Reggie Schwarz and Jack Mason. It could have been an example of country house cricket at its finest – except that there was no glut of runs on a plumb track in a match played under bright sunshine. Instead, rain before the match meant that the start was delayed on the first day until 2pm to allow the wicket to dry out and an absence of both wind and sunshine left the pitch soft and unreliable for strokeplay. Bosanquet himself made the top-score of 39 in a match in which all 40 wickets fell for just 553 runs. Although Herbert Baker, of Kent, took eight wickets for Robinson's XI, his haul was matched by that of the Hon Henry Mulholland, the current captain of Cambridge University.

Normal service was resumed with a string of comfortable victories over Norfolk clubs. The lower order of the CEYMS XI proved rather obdurate so Archie resorted to employing the 'lobs' of the elderly Charles Robson, who was much more used to keeping wicket. The move was instantly successful as Robson dismissed the last three men at a personal cost of a single run. Two of his victims were stumped by Archie in a rare appearance as the 'custodian'. Chasing only 134 and with time to spare, Old Buckenham Hall batted on once they had passed the CEYMS' total, as was the custom in those days; this allowed Mulholland, now appearing for rather than against Lionel's team, to show his credentials as an all-rounder for he pillaged an unbeaten 76 runs in just 45 minutes. Norfolk's new premier club, Norwich Wanderers, were then thrashed; Roderick Falconer and Conran bowled unchanged to dismiss the visitors for just 190, of which 109 were scored by Norfolk's premier batsman, Geoffrey Stevens, before Old Buckenham Hall racked up 304 for four. Archie made an unbeaten 150 whilst Dr Edmund Rose (a GP at nearby Attleborough and in all probability the Robinsons' family doctor) helped himself to 115.[44]

Following an equally convincing victory over Carrow, the next team up for ritual humiliation at the hands of Lionel were the Incogniti, who did not send a particularly strong team and should have known better. They held their own for the first half of a two-innings match but then found themselves overwhelmed by a double act of Eric Fulcher and Sid Pegler. The former made 97 and 57, also helping himself to eight wickets, whilst the latter scored 55 and 126, taking four wickets. In the face of those two outstanding players, the Incogniti went down by 207 runs, only their 'guest' player Conran doing himself justice; in the home team's second innings he returned figures of seven for 115, despite the *Eastern Daily Press* reporting that he received inadequate support from his fielders.

The first of the two first-class matches arranged for the year took place at the beginning of July, when Cambridge University visited for a 12-a-side fixture, their last before the Varsity Match.[45] Although Robinson's side contained four players with Test experience (Archie, Bosanquet, Pegler and Schwarz) the captaincy was entrusted to local all-rounder Michael Falcon. He was unsuccessful with the toss but saw his side asked to bat first. It had been reported that much work had been done on the wicket to produce a surface that Lionel would have approved of (it was reported that it had a 'glazed appearance, resembling the "cast iron" wickets of Australia') but a considerable amount of rain had fallen in the 24 hours before the match and it was expected that batting would be tricky on the first day. After a relatively good start, to which Bosanquet contributed 86, the university shuffled their bowlers and the sixth and seventh, skipper Mulholland and Freddie Calthorpe (every bit as 'Honourable' as his captain), each bagged four cheap wickets to dismiss Robinson's side for 195. In response, the Light Blues also found batting tricky and crumbled before the bowling of Falcon and Pegler; their ninth wicket fell at 102, at which point Eric Kidd came to the crease. It was reported that he was batting at 'jack' due to having a 'bad hand' but this did not seem to inconvenience him as he walloped 20 runs off the first six deliveries that he faced and finished on 34 not out when the innings closed at 139. On an improving wicket, Robinson's side batted more successfully in their second knock with Bosanquet passing 50 for the second time in the match, but they still only had 238 on the board when Archie, who had been sent in at number ten, was joined by the last man, Guy Napier. They added 69 runs in just 37 minutes, with MacLaren finishing unbeaten on 50, an innings described as 'splendid'. Set 364 to win, Cambridge seemed to be subsiding gently to defeat at 204 for eight with Barry Cumberlege having been persuaded not

---

44 In truth, the Wanderers were victims of some sharp practice. Knowing that the home team would probably be strong, they had hired the professional bowler Roderick Falconer for the afternoon to try and even things up. Apparently, Archie and Lionel found themselves a player short for once and, needing a bowler, shamelessly outbid the visitors for the services of Falconer who 'went over to the opposition'. His six wickets made a significant contribution to the home team's victory.

45 Cambridge were reputedly a strong batting side, having scored 609 for eight in their previous match, an innings defeat of the MCC.

to bat, to avoid aggravating a finger injury and so jeopardising his chance of playing in the Varsity match. However Kidd, now batting at number five, was then joined by Edward Baker and they, like Robinson's last pair, employed the 'long handle', adding 105 runs in 40 minutes. Opposing skipper Falcon went for 79 runs off his 11 overs and, at one point, Kidd and Baker hit 28 runs off nine deliveries. Eventually, Schwarz brought an end to the carnage and earned himself a five-wicket haul; Kidd was left stranded on 96.

That rarity, an away game, followed, with a strong team being sent to ensure victory over R.T.Fellowes' XI in the concluding match of that year's Honingham Cricket Week. Bosanquet then reappeared with the second of the two elevens that he brought to Old Buckenham in 1913 and Robinson was treated to a rarity that he will not have relished at all – his side getting a sound thrashing. Bosanquet's team batted consistently to make 293 and then shot out Hall for just 64. Following on, Hall did better, with Archie's 108 helping them to a total of 246, but the visitors knocked off the runs without loss. How Lionel would have fumed!

Following the scratching, for an unknown reason, of a game against the MCC, the season concluded with Old Buckenham Cricket Week, comprising of two three-day games. The first was a 12-a-side contest against the Oxford University Harlequins whilst the second was against J.R.Mason's XI. The fixture against the Harlequins was highly unusual in that, although Robinson's XI fielded a strong side containing six Test players, Lionel decided to play himself. This was only the third time he had taken the field that year; unlike Sir Julien Cahn he was reluctant to expose himself to ridicule by appearing in matches which were beyond him. For some reason this match proved to be an exception and was made even more noteworthy by the fact that he appears to have assumed the captaincy himself, ahead of both Archie and Johnny Douglas, once-and-future Test skippers. Robinson's XII batted first and were saved by Leonard Moon who scored 61 batting at number eight before becoming one of four victims of Teddy Wynyard's lobs. They eventually totalled 266, with skipper Lionel going in last and remaining proudly unbeaten with a single. Guy Napier then took six for 80 to restrict the Harlequins to 183. Disaster struck Robinson's team at the start of their second innings as they were reduced to 21 for four; a belligerent half-century from Aubrey Faulkner helped to alleviate the damage until Archie came in at number seven. He proceeded to plunder 141 runs in just 123 minutes, adding 94 in just over 45 minutes with Moon and 80 in 37 minutes with Schwarz. His innings was described as 'brilliant' and bowling figures suffered as a result: Francis Stocks conceded 91 runs in just 15 overs whilst George Cartwright saw 73 runs taken off his 12.1 overs. Lionel was thus able to declare at 300 for ten without having to bat a second time himself. Following Archie's innings it would have been a case of the swine chasing after the pearls. With a little application the Harlequins might have earned a draw but most of them batted poorly. The obvious exception was Bosanquet who launched an assault on the bowling to rival that of Archie. Batting at number five, he scored 108 in 110 minutes and was especially severe on the fast-medium of Douglas who took six wickets to bring his match haul to ten, but who conceded no fewer than 125 runs in just 23 overs. Bosanquet fought alone, however, and skipper Robinson had a comfortable victory to hang on his belt in what would appear to have been his last appearance as an active cricketer. His final record in those matches whose details have survived is a total of 143 runs in 29 innings, 20 of which were completed, for a batting average of 7.15. *CricketArchive* propose that a player named "LG Robinson" who turned out for W.G.Grace's XI against W.G.L.F.Lowndes' XI in a one-day fixture at Chesham in 1907 was the subject of this biography. This match would be of interest for it would be the earliest sighting of Lionel as a player. However, the player in question scored a sizeable 163 against an attack that included the Test star 'Old Jack' Hearne. It is inconceivable that this could have been the habitual duffer Lionel, but, just to make sure, Tom Walshe has been kind enough to obtain a picture of all the players involved and he assures me that none bears the remotest resemblance to Lionel.

The final match of the season, which was awarded first-class status, was between L Robinson's XI and J.R.Mason's XI, all eleven members of which represented Kent at some stage. Archie selected an extremely strong side to oppose them; eight had played, or would play, Test cricket (Bosanquet, Hendren, Moon, Pegler, Schwarz, George Gunn, Sydney Barnes and Claude Buckenham) and another, Frank Tarrant, who would certainly have done so if the regulations had been a little less strict than they were at the time. Not only was this eleven unusual in its strength, it was unusual in its social make-up – no fewer than five were extremely talented professional cricketers. This was not country house cricket in its strictest sense, where the result was of little importance, but a match in which the home side, at least, were determined to be victorious.[46] Having put a very strong side into the field, Robinson's eternal enemy, the weather, continued to frown upon Old Buckenham. A combination of heavy rain overnight and then drizzle on the day meant that the first day was completely washed out and play did not start on the second day until 2pm; even then a fresh pitch had to be cut. On the second afternoon Bosanquet's 74 helped Robinson's team to reach 236 for seven (five of the wickets falling to 'Daddy' Carr) at which point the innings was declared closed, a quixotic gesture as the match was already so far behind schedule for a result to be possible. At first, Mason's XI looked in little trouble and, largely due to the batting of Edward Humphreys and James Seymour, reached safety at 128 for two. However, the wicket was now beginning to offer something to the bowlers and, in Sydney Barnes, the home team had just the man to take advantage. He ran through the rest of Mason's batting, taking seven for 88 as the innings closed for 216. Robinson could thus claim first-innings honours. That was the end of the meaningful cricket; as many of the players needed to catch a train to attend the Scarborough Festival it was arranged to draw stumps as early as 4pm. After a desultory passage of play, in which

---

46   It was matches such as this that led Evelyn Metcalfe, whilst reminiscing on country-house cricket in *The Cricketer* in 1942, to suggest that Lionel had got rather carried away with the determination to win and had forsaken the true spirit of the country-house game.

Robinson's XI made 71 for five, the season at Old Buckenham came to a close. The *Eastern Daily Press* was kind to Lionel as usual, stating: 'The cricketing public owe a great deal to Mr Robinson for arranging such an attractive match.' However, the press omitted to mention that this match coincided exactly with the final of the Minor Counties Championship, between Norfolk and Glamorgan at the Lakenham County Ground; the date of Mason's visit had probably been arranged long before Norfolk topped the Minor Counties Table but the 'double-booking' probably looked to be a little incompetent and crowds at both venues would have suffered.

Only the most inattentive of readers can have failed to notice the name of Bernard Bosanquet cropping up again and again in the accounts of Lionel's matches in 1913. He appeared in no fewer than seven of the ten games played that season, missing only the three least important matches against local opposition. Apart from captaining his own elevens against Robinson's team twice (and winning both), he also represented the visiting Harlequins. Swapping sides, he played for Robinson against the Incogniti, Cambridge University, R.T.Fellowes' XI and J.R.Mason's XI. In his 12 innings he amassed 585 runs at an average of 48.75, scoring one century and four fifties. In a most successful season, he also took 15 wickets with his swervers, including a five-wicket haul against the Harlequins. He seems to have been one of Lionel's favourite guests, being of the right social class (he was educated at Eton), and a sound leader of men; Archie appointed him to skipper Robinson's teams in three of their six first-class matches.

1914: Sid Pegler takes the plaudits

When Archie sat down to organise the fixture list for the summer of 1914 he would not have expected the season to be cut short by the Great War. Therefore, one has to suppose that he arranged for a full programme of visitors to Old Buckenham, intended as lambs to be slaughtered on the altar of his employer's ambitions, only to be thwarted by the deterioration of the political scene during the summer. Whilst both the first-class and the Minor Counties Championship staggered on towards their scheduled conclusions, with a few fixtures being abandoned, country house cricket was more vulnerable and many matches were cancelled as the young men educated at public schools who provided the lifeblood of this form of the game hurried to enlist. In the end, Lionel Robinson found his season truncated so that he only had the chance to play host to six games; the final game that did take place as scheduled, against the locals of Garboldisham Manor, finished as early in the season as 25 July. The *Eastern Daily Press* noted that at least two fixtures (against the touring Philadelphians and the Oxford Harlequins) were cancelled and it is likely that further matches also went by the wayside, unrecorded.

What remained of the 1914 season started disastrously with a not particularly strong Old Buckenham Hall side going down to a crushing defeat of 148 runs (in a one-day match) by CEYMS. The visitors were largely indebted to Roderick Falconer, the Norfolk professional who had played for Northamptonshire, for their victory. He struck 61 runs, having been asked to open the batting but, when he was given the new ball, the chances of his team winning seemed small as a delayed declaration meant that Hall only needed to bat for 110 minutes to force a draw. However, Falconer (with six for 28) and F Hale (with four for 50) bowled unchanged to dismiss Hall for 84 in less than 20 overs and only 64 minutes. The match thus ended with plenty of time to spare and would have vexed Robinson considerably, especially as CEYMS were not out of the top-drawer of sides to visit Old Buckenham. Commenting on the game, the *Eastern Daily Press* reported: 'Lionel Robinson's fine ground presented an idyllic picture ... sylvan beauty ... A good easy paced wicket had been prepared by Porter, a Somerset man, till recently engaged on the Headingley ground staff at Leeds.'

A return to normal winning ways took place in the following two days when a much stronger Old Buckenham Hall side defeated the Incogniti by an innings and 28 runs. Although groundsman Porter failed to break his 'duck' batting at number eleven, the three players with Test experience all contributed significantly: Archie top-scored with 74, Jack Mason hit 64 and took five wickets in the game whilst Sid Pegler made 30 and finished with match figures of nine for 83. It was a classic piece of overkill committed upon hapless visitors, orchestrated by Archie to keep his employer happy and himself in a job. On 13 June Pegler again demonstrated why he was such a popular guest at Old Buckenham by striking 144 and taking six wickets in a Saturday afternoon thrashing of Carrow. This game was also notable for another appearance by Lionel's nephew, Lionel Frederick Robinson, who made little impression in scoring just four runs when asked to bat at number eight.

The highlight of the season was the visit of Oxford University for a first-class fixture at the start of July. This was the first time that the university, who were playing their last fixture before the Varsity match, had played a first-class match in the county. The wicket was described in the press as 'plumb' and as 'capital' and Oxford had no doubts about batting first when they won the toss. After Donald Knight and Miles Howell had batted well to put on 112 for the first wicket, their final total of 339 was slightly disappointing; Pegler, with a return of seven for 113, being largely responsible. Oxford would have felt much happier at the end of the first day's play because they dismissed both of Hall's openers, Archie and Kenelm McCloughin, for 'ducks' before the close. Then rain interfered with proceedings; only 110 minutes of play were possible on the second day during which Hall collapsed from nine for two to 129 for nine. Only Sir Timothy O'Brien, at the grand old age of 52, looked at all comfortable; he ended the day undefeated on 74, with his batting receiving rave reviews in *The Times*. Having made 144 in his previous innings at Old Buckenham, Pegler must have wondered why he had been put down to bat at 'jack' and had yet to go in. As it turned out the weather was much warmer and drier on the final day and the wicket rolled out well; O'Brien advanced his score to 90 before becoming Charles Rucker's fifth victim. He had taken only 100 minutes to compile his score and hit 14 fours. As Hall had conceded a deficit of 192 runs, it was no surprise that they were made to follow on. With Archie having been called away to Harrow on business,

Sir Tim O'Brien, the only man to make a first-class century for Lionel.
(Roger Mann)

captain Bosanquet promoted O'Brien to open and was rewarded with a fine century. O'Brien's 111 was not as rapid an innings as his first, lasting for 200 minutes, but, with hard-hit half-centuries from Jack MacBryan and the skipper, it meant that Hall reached the safety of 311 for seven at close of play.

CEYMS returned to Old Buckenham in late July and, having dismissed them for just 127 (largely due to a six-wicket haul by Roderick Falconer), Lionel Robinson must have been certain that revenge would be obtained for the drubbing that he had been forced to endure earlier in the season, especially as the CEYMS attack did not look formidable. However, 'Old George' Pilch took six for 54 and Hall were shot out for a mere 97 to lose by 30 runs on the first innings. There was enough time for Ted Gibson to take eight wickets 'at a small cost' when CEYMS batted again – however, the 'Churchmen' had secured a rare season's double over the Hall, albeit in two one-innings matches.

The team as a whole, and Pegler as an individual, returned to winning ways in the final match before the Great War. Hall batted first and, when their sixth wicket fell at only 188, Garboldisham Manor must have thought that they were in with a chance. However, Archie batted very well, making an unbeaten 128 and taking part in century partnerships for the seventh and eighth wickets with Evelyn Metcalfe (who scored 50) and Pegler (with

43) respectively. Pegler then took six for 54 and seven for 45 to dismiss Garboldisham Manor for 228 and 164. It was a match of two contrasting days; no fewer than 502 runs were made on the first day while only 11 wickets fell but, on a chilly and windy second day, the final 19 Manor wickets went down for just 303 runs. It finished an outstanding season for Sid Pegler; playing in the final five matches of the season he hit 235 runs at an average of 58.75 and also took 36 wickets - where bowling figures were available, his 29 victims cost just 10.17 runs apiece.

That proved to be the final match at Old Buckenham before the Great War. This would probably have caused little surprise at the time, given the political climate. However, what would have been surprising was that it also turned to be the end of regular country house cricket at Old Buckenham; it was widely expected that the war would be over by Christmas and it was probably assumed that Robinson would continue to bankroll cricket in 1915. As will be described in chapter five, when peace did eventually return in time for the 1919 season, there was no return to the salad days and very few high-quality matches were arranged at Old Buckenham.

Chapter Five:

The Great War – the end of Robinson's country house cricket

The Great War

Given that Robinson was past the age for military service and had only daughters, the onset of the Great War had no impact on his immediate family resident at Old Buckenham. However, his future sons-in-law, 'Jim Jack' Evans and John Graham Brockbank, and his nephew, Lionel Frederick Robinson, all served in the military and came through physically unscathed. Captain Evans, whose wedding to Viola took place at the Guards' Chapel in London's Wellington Barracks in 1916, was decorated with the Military Cross whilst serving with the Welsh Guards and was promoted to Major. Brockbank, who married 'Queenie' at Old Buckenham church in 1917, served in the Machine Gun Corps where he attained the rank of Lieutenant Colonel. Serving with great distinction in the navy, Lionel Frederick became a Lieutenant-Commander.

The Stock Exchange was closed at the end of July 1914 but, as stated in chapter one, Lionel did not resume activity on any significant scale when it reopened in January 1915. He spent the war years relatively quietly on his estate at Old Buckenham, the local press having more important things on which to report than the doings of a distant, rural outpost. In his obituary, Lionel Robinson was described as being 'Liberal and Imperialist in politics but .... not a frequenter of platforms'[47] so, in hindsight, it is not surprising that the Norfolk press failed to record him as a maker of jingoistic speeches. As will be described below, he preferred to express his support for the Allied cause by reaching into his pocket. His daughters were sighted in January 1915 when they invited local schoolchildren to tea in one of their father's larger buildings, the Foresters' Hall, which had been decorated for the occasion, but Robinson himself disappeared from view until October of that year when the residents of the parish of Wilby, of which he was lord of the manor, objected to a rate made for the relief of their poor by the Assessment Committee of Wayland Union and the Overseers of the parish. He instructed his lawyer, both to appeal against the rate, and to request that this appeal be deferred as there had been inadequate notice to prepare a case.

Soon afterwards, Robinson had need of his lawyers once more as he was taken to court by John Moon, a timber merchant who was seeking to recover £35 2s 6d for services rendered. The case was a complex one, dating back to 1914, but his barrister, Mr Claughton Scott, persuaded

---

47   Lionel was a member of the Reform Club in Pall Mall in central London, at one time the Liberal Party's unofficial 'headquarters'.

Judge Earley Wilmot to throw out the case.

Robinson served as the High Sheriff of Norfolk in 1916-17 but, again, the press was understandably more interested in chronicling the details of the next Big Push on the Western Front than in listing the engagements of the holder of a ceremonial post. Among the events that Robinson did attend as holder of the office was a service at Norwich Cathedral in August 1916 in memory of those men who had fallen in the second year of the war; the Lord Lieutenant (Lord Leicester) and the Lord Mayor also attended, as did around 50 wounded soldiers who had returned from the front. In October 1916 Robinson sat alongside the judge on the bench at the County Assize held at the Shirehall; he was accompanied by the Under Sheriff (P.E.Hansell) and by the High Sheriff's Chaplain (the vicar of Old Buckenham, Henry Anderson). It was reported merely that there were few cases to be heard.

During the Great War it was not uncommon for public schoolboys to aid farmers with their harvest so that the absence of farm labourers, who were away serving in the armed forces, would not seriously interfere with the collection of the crops. At harvest time in 1917, Lionel arranged with the National Service Committee for a party of about 30 senior boys from Downside (a school near Bath) to spend three weeks on the Old Buckenham

Lionel Robinson in ceremonial regalia as High Sheriff of Norfolk 1916.

Estate. Their job was to help Lionel's tenant farmers with whatever tasks needed doing; the farmers were distrustful at first but when the boys proved to be hard workers they were in great demand and jobs could have been found for double the number. At a rate of pay of fourpence an hour they certainly represented value for money. Unfortunately, the vagaries of the weather meant that their stay was slightly mistimed and they had to leave just before they would have been of maximum use. All the boys were members of the Officer Training Corps and the head of school was among them. Robinson originally housed them at his cricket ground, putting the pavilion and a marquee at their service but, when the marquee became flooded, he took half into the hall and placed the rest in his garage.

Lionel demonstrated his commitment to the Allied cause by financial rather than political gestures, being a conspicuously generous donor to many funds set up towards the end of the war. He donated £25 to the Edith Cavell Memorial Fund in May 1917 (with his wife contributing a further £10), and another £25 to the YMCA Hut Appeal Fund in October 1918; he responded to an appeal from Lady Leicester by gifting £50 to the 'Comrades Of The Great War Clubhouse Purchase Fund'.

After the Great War there was a great deal of correspondence in the *Eastern Daily Press* on what form war memorials should take. Some people favoured the erection of commemorative monuments whilst others proposed a more practical approach, with constructions in bricks and mortar being handed over to war veterans to use as they saw fit. There was no point in the residents of Old Buckenham starting up such a debate for Lionel Robinson, in a characteristic gesture of somewhat heavy-handed generosity, decided that he was going to pay for the entire project himself and, therefore, that the choice of the form that the memorial was to take was his alone to make. This made it highly unusual for the vast majority were financed through public subscription. The memorial that he chose was far from exceptional, however, in that the design was Sir Reginald Bloomfield's well-known 'Cross of Sacrifice', which was used in all the Imperial War Graves Commission cemeteries and at many other sites across Britain and its Empire.

The memorial, constructed on the village green of Old Buckenham, was unveiled by Mary Robinson on 31 August 1919. The octagonal base to the cross consisted of four levels upon which stands a tall stone cross with a bronze sword affixed. The names of those men of Old Buckenham who had fallen during the Great War were inscribed upon the base (with the names of those who fell during the Second World War being subsequently added). Among those listed as fallen were members of some of the families who provided players for the village cricket team (such as Bowen, Derisley, Gedge and Loveday).

Cricket after the Great War
It took several seasons for normal service to be resumed in English cricket. Many first-class players of note or potential had been wounded or killed and a significant number of young men were not demobilised immediately

The memorial given to Old Buckenham by Lionel after the Great War.
(Tom Walshe)

as the government deemed it necessary to keep sizeable forces in the Middle East and on the Continent. As well as replacing the 'lost' players, the authorities had to oversee the reconstitution of the structure of senior cricket. At Test level, the Australians were keen to resume Ashes tours as soon as possible but such was the damage done to the infrastructure of English cricket that it was not until 1926 that the Australians were seriously stretched and eventually defeated in a series.

At a lower level, school and club cricket also underwent a recuperative process. The area of the game where recovery was least successful and enduring was that of country house cricket. It is widely assumed that a disproportionate number of the upper-class men who had played this form of game before the war had perished while serving as junior officers on the Western front. It also seems clear that economic factors meant both that many of the surviving players now had to spend much more of their time in gainful employment rather than idling away their time in a succession of country mansions and that their one-time hosts no longer had the disposable income to provide a continuous stream of lavish hospitality to 22 young men of impeccable breeding.

To what extent this general picture applies to events at Old Buckenham is unclear. What is known is that Robinson, who had ceased to be active in the world of high finance but who still had a sizeable fortune, did not resume his bankrolling of country house games at Old Buckenham after the Great

War. The conventional view of the few cricket-lovers who have heard of Robinson at all, that he built a ground to first-class standard, funded a plethora of high-quality matches and was eventually rewarded with a game against the 1921 Australians is not so much a gross oversimplification as completely erroneous. By the time the tourists arrived in May 1921 the ground had reverted to being the home of a village cricket club, albeit one superbly equipped. In the two seasons of 1919 and 1920, between the recommencement of cricket at Old Buckenham after the war and the visit of the Australians, only two games of any significance were played on Robinson's ground. The first saw Robinson's XII take on the Australian Imperial Forces (AIF) in 1919 whilst the second was when Old Buckenham hosted the fixture between Norfolk and the MCC in 1920. The contrast with the pattern of games before the Great War, when matters can be described as quintessentially 'country house' is striking to say the least – but has gone completely unremarked upon by the local media. The most plausible explanation is that Robinson, ever a shrewd operator in matters financial, was husbanding his financial resources in the absence of any further significant income. [48]It is not exactly clear when Lionel first realised that he had little time left to live and it would only be possible to have the blindest of guesses as to how this might have affected his spending on cricketing matters.[49]

Keeping the flame alive

Although Robinson declined to bankroll any further country house cricket after the Great War, he made sure that his ground continued to be maintained to a first-class standard. Indeed, as has been noted in chapter two, Robinson was still actively engaged in improving the quality of his playing surface as he had turf especially imported from Australia. Unfortunately this event is as tricky to date accurately as the original laying out of the wicket involving Alec Hearne.

The fixture against the AIF constituted a dress rehearsal for the visit of the official Australian tourists two years later. The official visit had originally been planned for 1919 but had been cancelled and replaced by the AIF tour financed by the military authorities. Their tour of Britain was an extensive one, of 32 matches, 28 of which were deemed to be first-class and had the crowds flocking back to the cricket grounds after a four year hiatus. By the end of the tour, batsman Herbie Collins (who also replaced the prickly

---

48   That Robinson left nearly £250,000 in his will would mark him down as extremely wealthy by contemporary standards. However his nephew, Thomas Baxendale, responded to the details of Lionel's will by stating that 'he must have fallen on comparatively hard times if he only left £1/4m at his death'. Michael Robinson certainly remembers W.S. telling him that Lionel continued 'spending money furiously' during the war and commenting on 'how much money Lionel wasted on Old Buckenham Hall'. It might thus be possible to argue that, after the war, Robinson considered himself to be, by the standards of his family, somewhat of a pauper and that he cut his cloth accordingly when it came to spending vast amounts of money on cricket.

49   There is some evidence that Robinson could still 'splash the cash' in that, in September 1919, he hosted a match against a scratch eleven of servicemen raised by a Major Lister, who was stationed in nearby Pulham. For some reason he felt the need to call on seven players with first-class experience, who duly repaid him by defeating Lister's team by an innings. This could not have come cheaply and no-one apart from Robinson would have been at all interested in the result.

The AIF in the field 1919. They played their first match at Old Buckenham. (Roger Mann)

The AIF taking the field 1919 (left to right) W. L. Trennery, H. L. Collins, C. T. Docker (hidden), C. Kelleway, J. T. Murray, E. J. Long, A. W. Lampard, J. M. Taylor, C. B. Willis, J. M Gregory, W. S. Stirling. (Roger Mann)

Charles Kelleway as skipper after just six games), all-rounder Jack Gregory and keeper Bert Oldfield were all marked down for future greatness but when the side came to Old Buckenham the players were still just names for their match against Robinson's XII was the opening fixture of their tour.[50] They were opposed by a strong side containing seven players who had played Test cricket, or who would later do so, with the rest of the team being made up of cricketers from Kent – unsurprisingly Archie entrusted the captaincy to Jack Mason, now one of the grand old men of Kentish

50 Something seems to have gone amiss with the selection of Robinson's side for 12 players presented themselves for duty on the day. Luckily the AIF were amenable to playing a XII-a-side match and no-one was forced to drop out.

cricket. In unusually splendid weather, Robinson's XII made a very poor start, being bundled out for just 147 largely due to the pace bowling of Cyril Docker who took five for 34, but they managed to limit the AIF's lead on the first innings to 80. The bowling honours went to one of Lionel's tried-and-tested favourites, Sid Pegler, who took five for 54, whilst the leading batsman was Herbie Collins with 87. Facing that sizeable deficit Wally Hardinge dropped anchor and accumulated 72 runs in over three hours; at this point the tired AIF bowlers found themselves being battered by Lionel Troughton and Gerald Hough who added 124 in just 90 minutes for the seventh wicket. When Mason declared at 362 for eight, Hough was unbeaten on 87. As the AIF needed to depart early to travel to Leyton, where they were due to play Essex, it had been agreed to draw stumps at 3.30pm on the third day. This meant that the tourists had three hours and 45 minutes in which to score 283 on a pitch which was still playing well. Now it was the turn of Johnny Taylor to blunt the opponents' attack as he took over two hours to garner 66 runs; this paved the way for some more aggressive batting by Carl Willis and especially by Jack Gregory who hit 44 in just 40 minutes so that the AIF appeared to be coasting to victory. However, Frank Woolley managed to trap two batsmen with their pads in front of the stumps and the tourists lost momentum at a crucial time, slumping from 260 for six to 268 for nine. A few minutes later time was called with the AIF still nine runs short with two wickets in hand. At this point Lionel, in an unusually magnanimous mood, decided to risk defeat by having the match played out. Kelleway, however, declined his generous offer and the match was left drawn.

As usual, the *Eastern Daily Press* was full of praise for Lionel's ground, stating that: "[the AIF] will make the acquaintance of few, if any, better or prettier grounds than Mr Lionel Robinson's'. Plaudits were also accorded to the groundsman, providing evidence that the turf was still being lovingly maintained:

> *'The condition of the ground did Porter much credit. He did his bit in France and Mesopotamia, and has a shortened leg as a constant reminder of the great war, and in a few short months he, and his henchman, Squibs, brought the ground to a state of fitness that won praise from everyone. The wicket itself had that perfect appearance which draws a sigh from the bowler ...'*

The match between Norfolk and the MCC, which Lionel generously agreed to host, took place in August 1920. With Norfolk's regular skipper, Michael Falcon again busy in the House of Commons, Archie found himself captaining his adopted county for the only time.[51] His side was not the strongest for Michael Falcon, Geoffrey Stevens, Harry Falcon and Geoffrey Colman were all absentees; the MCC would have been pre-match favourites, having Test all-rounder Aubrey Faulkner and the highly-rated youngsters paceman Clem Gibson and leg-breaker Reg Bettington in their eleven. As usual, it rained on Lionel's parade and, despite play being allowed to continue until 7.20pm, there was only time on the first day for

---

51   During the Great War, Archie had served as a captain in the Royal Army Service Corps, before being invalided out in 1917.

the MCC to scramble to 138. On the second morning it was Norfolk's turn to bat on the far from dry wicket and they fared even less well than the MCC; apart from Eric Fulcher, who scored 47 at a run a minute, the only man to score more than six runs was the skipper who, having put himself in to bat at 'jack', made an undefeated 21. A final total of 89 left the home side with a deficit of 49. With runs being scarce and time running out, the MCC reached 59 for eight before declaring to set Norfolk 109 to win in 100 minutes. Norfolk made a much better fist of their second innings but three men were run out, most importantly the hard-hitting Harold Watson who had scored 24 runs before being dismissed. When stumps were drawn, the scores were level, with Norfolk having two wickets to fall – one of those was Archie, who was left stranded on 12. A most exciting finish!

The resurrection of the Old Buckenham Village Cricket Club
Whilst the ground at Old Buckenham was no longer in regular use for games of a high standard, Robinson was quite happy to let the reconstituted village club play on his square. Some of the players in this post-war club were survivors from the team which had played at Old Buckenham before Robinson's arrival and a perusal of Kelly's Directory of Norfolk for 1916 reveals that many of the family names of players in the cricket club are also found as occupants of the village (names such as Allington, Derisley, Gedge, Loveday and Whitehand). It would seem to have been a genuine village side, strengthened by the appearance of groundsman Porter, Harold Dougill (who went on to play in 18 games for the full Norfolk side), L.W.J. 'Len' Hart, and by the reappearance of 'Squibs'. It wasn't strengthened by the appearances of Lionel's sons-in-law; 'Jim Jack' Evans played once, without being asked either to bat or to bowl, while John Brockbank, who played six completed innings, only managed to break his 'duck' twice. Despite their assistance, the village side continued to prosper into the 1920s.

Len Hart – another forgotten man of Norfolk cricket
Leonard William John Hart, generally known as Len, was born in Thorpe St Andrew on 2 December 1888. He was one of five children born to William and Charlotte Hart; his father was a journeyman carpenter but Len was upwardly mobile and trained to become a schoolmaster. He married May Winifred Jackson in 1912, by which time it had already been established that he was an all-round sportsman. He would go on to excel at cricket, association football, golf, bowls and lawn tennis. Although his first serious sport was as a footballer playing for Thorpe Village Football Club, it was in cricket that he made his name, on and off the field. Hart's first teaching post was at Helhoughton, where he founded the Raynham and District Football League, but he was transferred to Old Buckenham in 1916. When the war ended he played a major role in the reforming of the village cricket and football clubs and it soon became clear that he was comfortably the best cricketer in the village eleven, for whom he turned out regularly. For the next few years, whether or not the village side was successful often depended on his personal performances with both bat and ball and he regularly took over 100 wickets in a season. It was Hart who was the

Old Buckenham CC 1920. Front, left to right: W 'Squibs' Groom, P Derisley, P Whitehand, LWJ Hart, H Loveday, S Loveday. (Back) Stella Frost, H. Petley, (unknown), P. Loveday, B. Gascoigne, G Stewart, V Allington (courtesy of Roger Wilson)

driving force behind the establishment of the South Norfolk Village Cricket League; at two meetings in March 1920 it was agreed that the competition be limited to genuine village clubs and no fewer than 21 teams applied to join in the inaugural year. Unsurprisingly, Old Buckenham were one of the teams that founded the League and Hart was unanimously elected to serve as secretary; he would also prove to be an automatic selection for the league's representative side. Lionel Robinson was asked to be president of the league and, at the end of the year, he permitted the league to play both its representative match against Honingham and District and the final of the league itself on his ground. At the conclusion of the final, Robinson gave a speech stating: 'Pulham was the best village team that he had seen play on that ground. There were some who said cricket was dying out, but he found that since the war there had been a great revival, and wherever the British flag was flown cricket and football were played.' Old Buckenham Hall continued to host important matches in the South Norfolk League for several years.

Hart was, however, ambitious to play at a higher standard than the South Norfolk League. Given that Robinson had more or less ceased to put out sides, Hart resorted to organising, and presumably captaining sides playing under his own name. These were stronger than the village side, although several of the villagers did turn out, but would have been no match for one of Robinson's teams – that the *Eastern Daily Press* deemed the results of his matches worthy of coverage indicates that Hart had been successful in escaping his humble beginnings. If there was no game to play in at Old Buckenham, Hart would turn out for other local teams such as Attleborough - he was clearly fanatically enthusiastic about playing. It has been suggested that he played so much cricket that it was a wonder that he could fit in the time to do any school-mastering; however the Norfolk Education Committee turned what the *Eastern Daily Press* described as a 'Nelsonian eye' to his absences and his son, Peter, claimed that his father's absences did not stop him being remembered as a 'damn good schoolmaster'. There happened to be a cricket-playing parson named Rev L.Hart based locally and Len would occasionally play under the name of the 'Rev Hart'; however, very few people were fooled by this somewhat transparent alias. Pupils remember Hart, dressed in his colourful South Norfolk blazer, letting them out of school early on match days so that he could return to his cricket. It has been proposed that his pupils would not have minded his absences for he was well-known to be something of a martinet in the classroom.

With Robinson ailing, but still alive, the facilities at Old Buckenham were under-used but once the owner passed away there was a vacuum in country house cricket which Hart and a few like-minded cricketers hurried to fill. In 1923 he was one of the founders of the South Norfolk Cricket Club, which was granted permission to base itself at Old Buckenham Hall by Lionel's widow Mary. Like Hart's own sides, South Norfolk were superior to the villagers in terms of social class and only Hart turned out for both elevens on a regular basis. They were also a much stronger team; inspection of the averages for the two teams in 1923 makes this amply clear, in that Hart was clearly still the dominant player in the village side but was just another member of the South Norfolk eleven. The story of how this club flourished and how Hart raised his game to become a highly effective bowler in top-quality club cricket will be dealt with in chapter seven.

Hart continued to arrange fixtures and play for the South Norfolk Club until their demise in the early 1930s more or less put an end to his career as an organiser of cricket and he returned to being merely a player, albeit a fanatically keen one. However the days of his greatest service to cricket in the county were still to come. In 1951 he took over the dual role of scorer and team manager for the senior Norfolk side and remained in post until he retired in 1967; he continued to visit Lakenham until failing eyesight in his last couple of years prevented him from attending. Serving under three skippers (Laurie Barrett, Peter Powell and Bill Edrich), Hart's obituary in the *Norwich Mercury* makes it clear that he was always ready to contribute ideas and to ask for better facilities for 'his' players. In the 1973 Norfolk annual report, Laurie Barrett referred to him as 'Uncle Len' as an indication of the affection with which he was regarded by 'so many young players'. His early years as a schoolmaster clearly prepared him for this role, although he had since switched careers and taken responsibility for organising the education classes at Norwich Prison.

In his final years, Hart lived in Plumstead Road East, Norwich with his second wife, Doris (nee Barber), whom he married in 1963 when aged

74. His obituary made it clear how highly Hart was regarded in Norfolk's cricketing circles, stating that he was 'one of the outstanding characters in Norfolk sport this century' and that 'it was as a personality that Len Hart impressed himself upon the .... world of Minor County Cricket in Eastern England.' The suggestion of the *Eastern Daily Press* to let 'Squibs' have the last word will be followed:

> *'Blast bor! There wunt be no cricket up the Hall without The Master. When he's on song with his owd leg breaks, yew'd betta keep yar eye in, dew yew 'ont last long!'*

Chapter Six:

The visit of the Australians in 1921 – the triumph of 'new money' at the eleventh hour

Armstrong's Australians

After the First World War the Australians pushed for an early resumption of Ashes tours, rather against the better judgement of the English authorities who felt that cricket in particular and society in general needed more time to recover. The Australians invited the MCC to tour in the winter 1919-20 but were rebuffed. It was felt impolite to refuse a second invite, so for the first official Ashes series after the war in 1920-21 the still reluctant MCC were induced to send a side captained by Johnny Douglas to play five timeless Tests against an eleven led by Warwick Armstrong. As is well known, England lost five-nil and were lucky to get nil. The English bowlers found the Australian wickets unreceptive and only Jack Hobbs of the batsmen consistently did himself justice. In paceman Jack Gregory and googly-merchant Arthur Mailey, Armstrong had two debutant bowlers

In 1921 Archie MacLaren strolls over the outfield at Old Buckenham with a friend who bears a striking resemblance to Neville Cardus - though there is no record of Cardus having attended the match. (PA)

who were far too penetrative (in their very different ways) for most of the visiting batsmen. So enthusiastic were the Australians to continue kicking the Mother Country while it was down that they had coerced the MCC into hosting another Ashes tour the very next English summer and the two teams travelled back to Britain on the same ship.

Although the outlook for English cricket fans did not look very rosy when Armstrong's team arrived, they were about to get much worse. One of the less highly considered of the tourists was the paceman, Ted McDonald; he had played in the final three Tests in the winter, capturing only six wickets at an expensive 65.33 runs each and was not regarded as a major threat. However, when he was given the new ball in the first match of the tour against Leicestershire, he demonstrated his liking for English conditions by taking eight for 41 and four for 63 as the hosts went down by the heavy margin of an innings and 152 runs. Before long he had formed a deadly new-ball partnership with Gregory which terrorised and rolled over batsmen in both county and Test matches.

The tourists at Old Buckenham

Before McDonald and Gregory could begin their country-wide rampage, they were obliged to visit Norfolk for their game against Lionel Robinson's XI. Archie, who had been more than willing to let other senior amateurs skipper his sides in previous important matches, decided that the opportunity was too good to miss and he decided to play in his first first-class match since 1914.[52] At this point the Australians had not started their 'reign of terror' so Archie had no reason to boast of how he could defeat them if only he was to be given a free hand. The game was thus of no more significance than any other warm-up game, except that Robinson was being represented by a particularly strong side.[53] The team was built about a core of established amateurs (Johnny Douglas, Donald Knight, Vallance Jupp, 'Jack' White and Percy George Fender)[54], some promising youngsters from Cambridge University (keeper George Wood, Clem Gibson and Percy Chapman) and a pair of the best professional batsmen that money could buy (Jack Hobbs and 'Patsy' Hendren, the latter playing his third first-class game at Old Buckenham Hall). Michael Down states that Archie had selected the team 'with the idea of fast-scoring, accurate bowling and, most important, brilliant fielding'.[55] It was a team described by Ronald Mason as being 'of all the talents', worthy of a festival match, perhaps at Scarborough, at the end rather than the beginning of the season and its positioning within the tour requires some brief consideration.

---

52 Before the match, Lionel was quoted as saying that Archie's presence as captain was worth 'a hundred runs'.

53 Lionel wrote to Pelham Warner to apologise that the match could not be used as an official Test trial, as Warner had requested, stating that his side had already been selected.

54 Archie had originally chosen Greville Stevens but he was unable to obtain leave from Oxford and was replaced by Fender.

55 Archie employed similar criteria when selecting his Eastbourne side; the main difference is that the team he selected to play at Old Buckenham was composed largely of Test-quality cricketers at or near their peak whilst the eleven selected for Eastbourne consisted almost entirely of 'long-shots', none of whom had caught the selectors' eye during the season.

Australia tour manager Syd Smith enjoying the hospitality at Old Buckenham Hall in 1921. (Sydney Smith Collection, State Library of NSW)

Play under way in 1921. (Sydney Smith collection, State Library of NSW)

Successful though Archie MacLaren had been in arranging six first-class games in his six seasons as Lionel's manager of cricket, he had always to squeeze his fixtures in to suit the schedules of his prospective guests rather than being able to present his employer with top quality matches at the height of summer. Hence the 1912 South Africans and Jack Mason's XI both visited in the festival month of September whilst the games played by both universities against Robinson's teams were their last before the all-important Varsity matches – conversely Lionel had to content himself with hosting both the AIF and the 1921 Australians at the start of their tours. Beggars, even exceedingly rich ones, cannot be choosers. Gideon Haigh professes to being puzzled by the existence of the fixture at all, stating that: 'How [Robinson] had insinuated a traditional country house match into the Australian team's crowded schedule is a mystery; it is a fair guess money played a large part.' Ronald Mason is a little more cryptic, describing the fixture as 'somewhat ambiguous'.

It is indeed unclear quite how Lionel managed to secure the visit to Old Buckenham by the 1921 Australians; it may be that strings might have been pulled at an extremely high level. In the Victorian era the organisation and financing of Ashes tours were generally carried out by the tourists themselves and wealthy cricket-lovers such as Lionel had chances of "buying" a fixture. However, in the years before the Great War, the MCC and its counterpart, the Australian Board of Control for International Cricket (ABCIC), muscled in and assumed the rights to administer all future tours, rights they guarded jealously. This signalled the end for the likes of Lionel and the match at Old Buckenham in 1921 remains the only match granted first-class status that the Australians have played on a "country house" ground since that War. As such it was something of a "living fossil", a throwback to earlier times that demands further explanation. That the two captains, Archie and Warwick Armstrong, were close friends would have facilitated the organisation of the match once it had been arranged but neither was in a position to exert sufficient influence to bring it about in the first place. Armstrong had been defeated in his power struggle with the ABCIC, and particularly with Syd Smith, the man appointed to manage the 1921 tour, whilst Archie was a maverick; although not exactly persona non grata at Lord's, he was not particularly persona grata either. Michael Robinson has pointed out that the impetus to accommodate Lionel's match into a busy tour may well have been provided by his brother, WS, who: "had a very close relationship" with the Australian Prime Minister, Billy Hughes, and also: "had an important relationship with the British Prime Minister, Lloyd George and in particular with the then Chancellor of the Exchequer, Lord Horne...". Without going as far as identifying WS as a significant mover-and-shaker in arranging the Australians' visit to Old Buckenham, Michael states that: 'These connections would not have been unhelpful to Lionel in connection with his proposed 1921 cricket match.' Whether or not WS was indeed involved, influence of the magnitude that he was able to wield would seem to have been necessary to bring about "Lionel's coelacanth" in the face of the usual institutional lack of enthusiasm for private enterprise demonstrated by the cricketing authorities. This is not to contradict Gideon Haigh, however, for significant amounts almost certainly changed hands, with the tour manager, Syd Smith, being the obvious point of contact to help things happen for Lionel. Smith himself implicitly denies this; in his thorough book chronicling the tour he includes a copy of the accounts and these disclose that Lionel Robinson handed over a mere £150 to the tourists. To put this into perspective, the Australians generally received three or four times this "fee" as their share of receipts from a first-class tour match, with fixtures against well-supported counties (such as Surrey, Middlesex, Yorkshire and Kent) bringing in over £1,000 each and the Tests even more. Robinson even appeared to pay out less than Cumberland, whose one-day match is listed by Smith as costing them £160. Even when Lionel's generous hospitality is taken into account it is clear that Smith is asking posterity to believe that the tourists agreed to shoehorn a three-day trip to Old Buckenham into a packed schedule for an absolute pittance. Most unlikely! Alas, more than ninety years on, one can but speculate about such matters but it seems probable that the Australian cricketers and their manager will have "found" some crisp bank notes awaiting them in their bedrooms. The friendship between the two skippers could well have aided the reaching of an agreement as to who received exactly how much "boot money". The taxman failed to find out and so shall we.

The first day was an almost total anticlimax as the weather was as uncooperative as one might have feared for a game starting as early as 4 May. There were barely 15 minutes of play, starting at noon, as heavy rain and even snow prevented much activity; the tourists barely had time to open their innings after Armstrong had won the toss and decided to bat. Even though a north wind meant that it was also extremely cold[56], a hopeful crowd of around 2,000 attended; many were brought from the station by a non-stop convoy of ponies-and-traps organised and paid for by Lionel but many arrived by motor car, as did the players. Play was not abandoned for the day until 4.15pm but it is not clear how many souls were both hardy and optimistic enough to remain until that point.

On the second day (which was dry but still windy and chilly) the Australians continued to bat but made only 136 (which would turn out to be their lowest score of the tour). They started uncertainly and then collapsed totally, their last six batsmen accumulating just 13 runs between them. Only skipper Armstrong, with an unbeaten 51, compiled over 100 minutes, put up much of a fight. They didn't have to bat on a typically quick Old Buckenham wicket; the strip used was described as 'none too easy' but it was far from spiteful and 136 was clearly a below par score. There had been fears that the wicket would turn into a difficult, drying one on the second day but these worries turned out to be unfounded. Obtaining late swing in both directions, Johnny Douglas led the attack and bowled unchanged to end with figures of six for 64; Clem Gibson's fast-medium

---

56   It was so cold that Charlie Macartney, who was being billeted at the Royal Hotel in Attleborough, appealed to Lionel for some coal as, with a coal strike on, the hotel was freezing. As would be expected, Lionel responded instantly and a half a hundredweight of coal was carried back to Attleborough 'in high glee'.

outswingers providing support as he took three for 33. The fielding lived up to expectations, with Chapman's catch off a hard cut by Hendry coming in for special mention. In a spell of nostalgia, *The Times* paid tribute to Archie's captaincy in the field:

'It was good to see Mr MacLaren leading a side again; there was the same genius displayed in the placing of the field, the same skill in blocking the batsman's favourite stroke, while one beautiful pick up with the left hand in the slips served to remind us that he still retained his skill as a slip fieldsman.'

The wicket remained a little tricky when Robinson's XI went in, lending assistance to Ted McDonald's break-backs and to Gregory's pace. After the early departure of Donald Knight, Hobbs and Jupp took the battle to the Australian attack, with the former being the dominant partner until the latter overcame a shaky start. Hobbs took a couple of blows from shortish deliveries but seemed untroubled. In Leo McKinstry's comprehensive biography of 'The Master', he is described as showing 'precise judgement in leaving the ball, playing a dead bat or going on the attack'. Ronald Mason, who has a pretty turn of phrase, stated that: 'Hobbs ... tamed the fast openers and ... was the complete and prolific master of Mailey; he batted with the rare grace and control that only a great batsman can command against bowlers who begin with a high psychological advantage ... Hobbs, the quick-footed hawk-eyed master, playing [Gregory and McDonald] both like fish on the end of the line.' He then continued his purple prose: 'It is to be doubted if 1921, during all its blistering iron-hard summer, ever saw a finer concentration of cricket as it did in the depths of Norfolk, for an hour or two, on this cold uncertain May afternoon.' As was stated in the Introduction, Mason had little time for Lionel Robinson's cricket and

Herbie Collins batting on the third day at Old Buckenham.

Jack Hobbs faces Ted McDonald.
(Sydney Smith collection, State Library of NSW)

it is implicit in his coverage of this match that Old Buckenham was an unworthy scene for an innings that Jack Hobbs himself thought might have been the best of his life.[57] Len Hart, who had helped organise the fixture, accommodated the professionals Jack Hobbs and Patsy Hendren during the match and, many years later, Hobbs confirmed to Hart that his unbeaten 85 was indeed one of the high points of his career, stating that: 'They made me fight for every run.' Similarly, in an interview given to *The Times* in 1952, Hobbs was quoted as saying: 'I was playing at my best form. I always think that I hit the real height of my abilities. Everything came off. There were some good bowlers and all my shots I kept middling, everything in the middle of the bat.' At the time, Warwick Armstrong regarded this innings as one of the best played against his side during the whole tour; that he did not feel inclined to put himself on to bowl at all remains something of a mystery, but he might have observed how Hobbs had made a complete mockery of the bowling of Armstrong's fellow-spinner Arthur Mailey and thought better of it.

The majestic display only ended when Hobbs had to retire hurt, having made 85 of the first 125 runs. He re-aggravated the strain of a thigh muscle which he had originally damaged in Australia the previous winter; Jupp stated that he could hear the tissue snap as they stole a quick single. 'The Master' was helped back to the pavilion, clearly in great pain. Jupp continued to bat until the close; partnered by Hendren he took the score to 156 for one at close. When compared to the batting of Hobbs, the contribution of Jupp has tended to be overlooked, but his innings of 59 was also skilfully compiled and of great merit. His thumb (or possibly a finger) had taken a battering from the Australian pace attack and he

---

57   Indeed Mason sees this match as important only in the fact that Jack Hobbs suffered the serious injury which ruled him out of the first two Tests; going so far as to state: 'What became of the match after [Hobbs' injury], nobody cares.' To an extent, Haigh takes a similar view.

was unable to resume his innings on the third morning. Despite Percy Chapman failing to survive the first ball of the day, Robinson's side advanced their score to 256 for eight before declaring on the final day; Douglas contributed significantly with a dogged but unbeaten 41 in nearly two hours and Archie struck five majestic boundaries batting at 'jack'. There was just time for the tourists to crawl to 25 for one before play was brought to a close by rain (as usual) after lunch with stumps being finally drawn at 4.15pm. The Australians were severely harassed by the bowling of Gibson, who returned the impressive figures of 9-8-1-1, again on a pitch that was far from malicious.

As Robinson always allowed the public free admission to games at Old Buckenham Hall, it is not possible to be very clear about how many spectators watched play on the second day. Estimates vary between a low of 5,000 to 6,000 from the local press to a high of 12,000 with, perhaps, 10,000 being a popular compromise. The frequently negative Ronald Mason took the rosiest view of all: 'Twelve thousand people saw it; they are among the world's most fortunate mortals.' The press in general was allowed a rare moment of optimism before the Australian juggernaut gathered momentum and all but destroyed English cricket; a typical comment ran: 'Yesterday proves that the Australians can be dismissed cheaply ... the plain fact is that they were fairly and squarely outplayed.' (This comment appeared in the *Daily Express*, which was the paper Archie wrote for.)

Although two out of the three days' play ended in damp anticlimax, there was no doubt that the quality of the home team's play on the second day meant that the match as a whole was a triumph for the dying Robinson. The ground earned its usual plaudits in both local and national press, being described as 'picturesque' by more than one journalist, with the *Eastern Daily Press* claiming that 'there are few, if any ... better kept grounds in the kingdom'. Groundsman Porter received his usual honourable mention but here Archie, rather than Lionel, was cast in the role of groundsman's assistant. (In passing, the ground was described as the second laid out by Lionel Robinson at Old Buckenham; the subject of the first ground will be returned to in chapter seven). *The Times* waxed most lyrical:

> *'All lovers of cricket in England should be grateful to Mr Robinson in that he has given our visitors a chance of playing a match in a typical English country house. It must be remembered, too, that at Old Buckenham Hall there is the most perfect little cricket ground, with a magnificent wicket and a glorious outfield. Although it is country house cricket, yet it is cricket of a most serious nature, and, of course, ranks as a first class fixture. Mr Robinson therefore, has got together a side worthy of his opponents, and great credit is due to him for this genuinely helping the English Selection Committee.'*

Even Mason, the severest critic of Robinson's match in theory, forced himself to write a few kind words stating that the fixture was 'a happy memorial to the founder of the feast, Mr Lionel Robinson' and, further, that: 'We owe him a lot.' Lionel and Archie would have been pleased and

Jack White bowled by Jack Gregory.

the former marked the occasion by presenting each player with a tie in his racing colours, described by Herbie Collins as 'my ideal tie'.

The prophet crying in the wilderness
Having got very much the better of the Australian tourists, and fielding a strong side, Archie felt entitled to blow his own trumpet at every opportunity. During the summer that followed the Australians' visit to Old Buckenham, English cricket suffered from a widespread defeatism that had been born in the whitewash that they had suffered the previous winter. Most people forgot the events at Old Buckenham, but not the ex-England skipper. Mason, describing the match as 'a curious and interesting portent', states that Archie 'maintained stoutly through the hell and high water that engulfed England during the next few months that this, and not the succeeding matches, represented Australia's true quality, and nothing of the horrors to come could persuade him that they were not vulnerable if the proper team to beat them could be assembled'. He began his verbal campaign as early as the aftermath of the first Test, admittedly an utter shambles for the home side, giving 'all the English team a considerable roughing-up in an article published just before the second Test ... whereas most critics found the displays of Knight and Holmes a twin consolation ... [he] found a whole string of faults in each of them and criticised their footwork and technique without mercy. There seems ... much sound sense in what [he] said; though there is a hint or two that there were those who were disposed to convict him of rocking the boat.'

Michael Down reports: 'Throughout the season the man who was so often branded a pessimist took every opportunity to speak up for English prospects, as long as the correct players were chosen. He pressed the claims of the younger generation but such calls were ignored by the selectors.'

Archie did a fair amount of socialising with the Australians during their tour; before he died, tourist Hunter Hendry told Michael Down that, when their itinerary found them in London, they were based at the Cecil Hotel and MacLaren, accompanied by his boozing chum Walter Brearley, would frequently visit them to ask their opinion of the various county players that they had encountered during their travels – possibly seeking information that would help him select his side to play the tourists at Eastbourne.[58] There seems to have been a fair bit of good-natured banter, with Archie suspecting the tourists of extravagantly praising British cricketers that they would actually be pleased to see selected to appear against them in the Tests.

Having been given his chance, Archie wrote to Neville Cardus: 'I think I know how to beat Armstrong's lot; come and write about it for *The Guardian.*' Cardus, ever the romantic, took his lifelong hero at his word and persuaded his reluctant editor to let him cover the match at Eastbourne rather than the fixture between Surrey and Middlesex, the result of which would decide the County Championship. No other cricket journalist of note had paid much attention to Archie's rattling of his sabre and Cardus found that he was the only reporter from a national as opposed to a local paper in the press box when the match commenced.

Archie's Triumph at Eastbourne
The story of Archie MacLaren's eleven's struggle to defeat the previously invincible 1921 Australians is one of the most heroic in English cricket lore. Although Lionel Robinson was not actually present at the match at Eastbourne, Ronald Mason is undoubtedly correct in attributing its

Johnny Douglas batting, Mailey fields.
(Sydney Smith Collection, State Library of NSW)

---

58   It was not until August that Archie discovered that he had been granted his wish and awarded *carte blanche* to organise and skipper 'An England XI'.

genesis to the visit of the Australians to Old Buckenham earlier in the season and a brief description of what Jeremy Malies has described as 'the most romantic match in the history of the game' [59] will serve as a coda to Robinson's career as a financier of high quality cricket.

Given an absolutely free hand to pick whoever he wanted, Archie chose to base his team almost entirely on current or former Light Blues. In June, he made the short journey from Old Buckenham to watch Cambridge take on the tourists and though the university was soundly thrashed by an innings and 14 runs, he saw enough potential to select six of the current Blues. The three Ashton brothers and Percy Chapman provided a nucleus of fast-scoring batsmen who were also brilliant fielders and Clem Gibson and leg-spinner 'Father' Marriott were quality bowlers. The Light Blue contingent was completed by keeper George Wood (who, with Gibson and Archie himself, were the only survivors from the match at Old Buckenham) and by Michael Falcon, a classy paceman who had been unlucky not to be selected for at least one Test but who was now over 30 and completely out of practice owing to his duties as an MP. To complete his team Archie selected Geoffrey Foster, a competent but not outstanding batsman who had been a Dark Blue many years before, and Aubrey Faulkner, who once had claims to be the best all-rounder in the world but who, like Falcon, seemed to be past his 'sell-by' date (and who was neither remotely fit nor even English). Ronald Mason (him again!) described Archie's selection as 'an interesting, gay, random, attractive, hugely vulnerable side'. It became even more vulnerable when Marriott had to cry off due to illness and Archie drafted in his boozing mate, Walter Brearley, who had won four

Lionel Robinson with the Australian team.

<hr />

59   Warwick Armstrong's biographer, Gideon Haigh, agrees with Malies, referring to it as 'one of the century's most celebrated matches'.

AUSTRALIA

Match Between BUCKENHAM HALL ATTLEBORO AND TUNBRIDGE ROBINSON'S XI.

ON MAY 4, 5, 6 1921

FIRST INNINGS OF AUSTRALIA 4, 5, 6

Order.	Batsmen.	Runs as Scored.	How Out.	Bowler.	Total Balls rec'd	TOTAL
1	Bardsley, W		c Whit.	Douglas		10
2	Collins, H. L.		c Knight	Gibson		23
3	Macartney, C.		c Wood wkt	Douglas		11
4	Taylor, J.		Run Out			20
5	Armstrong, W		Not Out			51
6	Gregory, J.		l.b.w	Douglas		2
7	Ryder, J.		c Knight — nlys	Douglas		0
8	Hendry, H.		c Chapman — cght	Gibson		5
9	Carter, H.		c Topp wkt	Gibson		2
10	McDonald, E		l.b.w	Douglas		0
11	Mailey, A		l.b.w	Douglas		4
	BYES 11	LEG BYES 3		WIDES.	NO BALLS.	8
					TOTAL	136

RUNS AT FALL OF EACH WICKET.

1	2	3	4	5	6	7	8	9	10
28	39	53	103	106	116	125	127	128	136

RETIRING BATSMEN.

The scorecard for the Australian first innings. Note the drawing in the top left corner. (courtesy of Melbourne Cricket Club Library)

AUSTRALIA

Match Between L. ROBINSON'S XI.

Buckingham Hall.

AND

ON May 4, 5, 6

INNINGS OF English XI. FIRST

Order	Batsmen	Runs as Scored	How Out.	Bowler.	TOTAL
1	Hobbs J.		Retired hurt	bowler.	85
2	Knight D.J.		L.B.W	McDonald	1
3	Tapp P.C.W		Retired	Gynal bowl	59
4	Hendren E.R.		c Hendry	McDonald	20
5	Chapman A.P.F.		c Hendry	McDonald	0
6	Douglas J.W.		Not Out		41
7	Fender P.G.		c Hendry	McDonald	10
8	Wood G.E.C.		c Gregory	Hendry	2
9	Gibson C.H.		c Mailey	Gregory	1
10	White J.C.		Bowled	Gregory	0
11	MacLaren A.C.		Not Out		25
	BYES 8	LEG BYES 2	WIDES,	No. BALLS, 11	12
				TOTAL	256

RUNS AT FALL OF EACH WICKET.

RETIRING BATSMEN.

Dot under Batsman's Score indicates a Chance.

The 'English XI' first innings card, showing opener Jack Hobbs retired with a 'bad leg'.

Bowling Analysis.

Bowler.		1	2	3	4	5	6	7	8	9	10	11	12	13	14	15	16	17	18	19	20	Overs.	Maidens.	Runs.	Wides.	No Balls.	Wickets.	Average.
Gregory																						13	2	45			2	
Mc'Donald																						25	4	62		2	4	
Macartney																						6	1	18				
Hendry																						30	10	73			1	
Mailey																						6		46			1	

Date,
Score on.
Time on.
Score off.
Time off.
Overs from.
Overs to.
Wides.
No Balls.

The Australian bowling analysis.

Test caps before the Great War as a genuine 'quickie', but who was now 47. According to Jeremy Malies, Arthur Mailey thought the sight of the old-timers practising was hilarious and chortled: 'Archie, old boy, you haven't got the Bolter's chance.'

The weather on the first day was warm and sunny and the Saffrons wicket perfect so it was no surprise that, when Archie won the toss, he decided to bat. An eager crowd of about 9,000 looked on aghast as MacLaren's team were dismissed for a totally shambolic 43, Ted McDonald and Warwick Armstrong each bagging five wickets. To seal Archie's fate (or so it seemed at the time) Walter Brearley pulled a leg muscle while batting so that Archie was left with just three bowlers.[60] Apparently though, he rose to the occasion magnificently and led his team in the field as if confident of eventual victory. When the Australians reached 80 for one, this did not look at all likely but Falcon and Faulkner suddenly upped their game and each produced a superb spell of bowling which caused the tourists to collapse to 174, a lead of 131. Falcon recorded figures of six for 67, performing as well against the tourists as any bowler had all season, while Faulkner supported him with four for 50.

With only a few minutes left in which to bat, Archie decided to employ two nightwatchmen and unselfishly chose to open with himself and George Wood. The keeper failed to last until the close and, when Archie fell to the first ball of the second day, things were continuing to look grim. The score was taken on to 60 for four when the match was turned on its head by a partnership of 154 in three and a half hours between Hubert Ashton, who was finally dismissed for 75, and Aubrey Faulkner who went on to reach a magnificent 153. By the end the tourists were run ragged; they conceded 326 runs with Mailey and Gregory in particular failing to take any wickets between them despite having 127 runs taken off their bowling. This left the tourists a target of 196 for victory and there was just time for the Australians to reach 25 for the loss of Herbie Collins before stumps were drawn. For the first time since the start of the match, Archie was not the only person on the ground who thought that his team had a chance of victory.

The third and final day's play appeared to have been as keenly fought as any Test match with the grimly determined Australian batting line-up forced to fight for every run against accurate, hostile pace bowling and superb fielding, expertly orchestrated by Archie from slip. Gibson in particular bowled finely but, when Falcon finally tired after having kept up an accurate barrage for an innings and a half, the tourists sensed victory. Archie, still exuding confidence, made the only change open to him, bringing on Faulkner, and the South African leg-spinner rewarded him by aiding Gibson to hurry through the Australian's middle and lower order, dismissing them for just 167 and giving the England XI victory by 28 runs. Fittingly, Armstrong was one of the last to resist but he was not particularly adept at facing high-quality leg-breaks and Faulkner duly

---

60   Brearley did try to bat in the second innings but had to employ a runner. Inevitably, he was run out.

trapped him leg before wicket.

Despite the intensity of play on the final day, hard-nosed cynics might still state that this was a meaningless victory over a side who were, to quote Ronald Mason 'dog-tired ... by the ... grinding routine [of touring]' and who might not have been that interested in the result. He further describes that the normally truculent Armstrong made a most magnanimous speech to the Eastbourne crowd after the match, which could be taken as evidence that the Australian skipper was not unduly concerned. E.H.D.Sewell wrote otherwise, stating that: 'Armstrong was simply livid at the result. He galumphed down to the station alone like a wounded bear with a very sore head, extremely tired of life, and scarcely on speaking terms with the rest of his team!'[61] After the two disastrous Ashes series, the result at Eastbourne was seized upon by English cricket-lovers desperate for any sort of success. It was acclaimed as a great victory and meant that Armstrong's team was unable to describe itself as 'invincible', unlike Bradman's tourists of 1948.[62]

It was an outstanding day for Archie and his team, particularly Faulkner, Falcon, Gibson and Hubert Ashton. In the heat of the moment the plaudits were for Archie, described as 'calm and dignified' by Gilbert Ashton, and no-one remembered that a major causal factor in the nemesis of the tourists was Robinson's pound.

Warwick Armstrong cover drives a boundary at Old Buckenham, watched by (left to right) Percy Fender, Percy Chapman, Archie MacLaren and George Wood.

61 The literally sore heads were found the next morning and belonged to Archie, Faulkner and Brearley, who celebrated their victory by drinking themselves under the table.

62 It is amusing that Bradman was only too aware of the dangers of his team losing the unbeaten record that he so coveted at the hands of a very strong side masquerading as a 'festival' eleven that he stipulated that only a limited number of Test-class players should oppose his team in such fixtures. This approach would have been useless against Archie's team with its total of no current Test players.

Chapter Seven:
The death of Lionel Robinson and the
fate of his cricket ground

The last rites

As Armstrong's team left Norfolk, their collective tail somewhat between their legs, the atmosphere at Old Buckenham must have resembled that of a town that has just seen the circus depart. The feeling that an era was coming to a close can only have been increased when the press announced that there would be a sale at the Royal Hotel, Norwich, on Saturday, 6 August when a John D Wood would be offering up for sale numerous sporting and agricultural property from the Old Buckenham estate as well as nearly 900 acres of land, a sizeable part of Robinson's domain. Alas, if Lionel was in dire need of money, it was not forthcoming as many items were withdrawn, unsold. As was stated in chapter five, neither Lionel's physical health nor the state of his bank balance were conducive to the resumption of country house cricket on any significant scale and it is a clear sign of his lack of further ambitions that he dispensed with Archie MacLaren. Archie returned to life on the breadline. He started by taking a coaching engagement at Lancashire, but his undiplomatic manner meant that he was released after only two years' service. In later years he had to turn his hand to keeping a hotel (where, perhaps unsurprisingly, he was too rude to his guests for his own good), to importing willow from Spain to make cricket bats and to further coaching, a role in which he made innovatory use of films that he had commissioned. He returned to the management of cricket tours, captaining the MCC tour to Australia and New Zealand in 1922-23 (where he brought his first-class career to an end with an unbeaten double century at Wellington) and overseeing the visit of S.B.Joel's XI to South Africa in 1924-25. He also revived his career as a journalist, writing regularly for *The Cricketer* in the 1920s and 1930s and published two instructional volumes on cricket. In the mid 1930s, his wife Maud inherited a sizeable fortune and they were able to retire, building an estate on 150 acres near Bracknell and playing the bountiful hosts, rather as Archie's ex-employer, Lionel Robinson, had done before him.[63]

Only one more match was arranged in the summer of 1921 and that too involved hosting a set of international tourists; this time the Philadelphian Pilgrims, the fourth fixture of whose tour involved them visiting Old Buckenham in early August for a two-day match.

---

63   In 1938 he journeyed to Hollywood to visit Sir C Aubrey Smith, who had also skippered England at Test cricket, and was not too proud to take a walk-on part behind Smith, who was starring in Alexander Korda's film, *The Four Feathers*; he appeared as a veteran of the Crimean War and was paid two guineas for two days' work. Archie died of cancer in 1944 at the age of 72.

Robinson had often seemed to be unlucky with the weather and this match was more affected than many. The ground was reported to be in good condition but sufficient rain fell during the first day that a fresh wicket had to be cut and play extended until 7pm to make up for lost time. Having collapsed to 100 for seven, the Pilgrims recovered to close on 158 for no further loss. Unfortunately there was even more rain during the night and, when the next day brought both sunshine and wind, the inevitable result was to transform the wicket into a 'sticky dog' on which batting was highly problematic. After the tourists' tail had wagged and lifted their score to 213, Robinson's team were shot out for just 124. Only Gerald Hough, with an attacking 69, could do anything with the Pilgrims' attack. When the Philadelphians went in again, they too floundered; only two men reached double figures as they stuttered to 98. Robert Fowler took full advantage of the conditions to return match figures of 11 for 106. There was only time remaining for Robinson's XI to reach 51 for three before a draw was agreed at 6.40pm. The *Eastern Daily Press* was somewhat critical of the Americans, stating that the wicket was still sufficiently treacherous that they should have declared their second innings closed and given themselves more time to bowl out the home team. In their defence, it is not clear how much experience they had at playing on an English 'sticky dog'.

Whilst the 1921 season saw little high-quality cricket in Old Buckenham, the village club continued to play in the South Norfolk League with no little success; they reached the semi-final but had their dreams of glory rudely shattered when Garboldisham bundled them out for an embarrassing total of 20. Lionel permitted them to play most, if not all, their home games on his ground, with the most noteworthy performance of the season being Len Hart's dismissal of five Thetford batsmen with five consecutive balls. Although Old Buckenham failed to reach the final of the league, Lionel again hosted that fixture and, when presenting the Cup to Garboldisham, he stated 'how pleased he was to see the final played on his ground'.

The following season took place under a cloud for it was now common knowledge that Robinson was terminally ill with cancer and unlikely to survive the summer. Activity of a cricketing nature at Old Buckenham centred almost entirely on the village club. Although a press strike affected coverage of local cricket in Norfolk and obscures historical research, it is clear that the local team was less successful than previously and they failed to reach the knock-out phase of the South Norfolk League. Only two other games appear to have taken place at the Hall ground that year; an unimportant match involving one of Len Hart's eponymous elevens and Lionel's final country house match, a two-day fixture against Australia House on 3 and 5 June. Although the home team was not notably strong (skipper George Wood, who also kept wicket, was the only 'big' name and space was found for several local cricketers, including John Brockbank, who made his usual 'duck's egg'), several players had some first-class experience and the side was far too strong for the visitors. Lionel's last match was thus one of those overwhelming victories that he enjoyed so much. Australia House won the toss and chose to bat, but were rolled over for just 66 in a mere 70 minutes, their innings lasting for just 18 overs. This was largely due to the bowling of Desmond Roberts who took six for 37. When Lionel Robinson's XI batted they ran up the relatively huge total of 355, with Norfolk's George Neville scoring 104 and Colonel Lancelot Ward 84. Australia House did slightly better in their second innings but their score of 110 meant that they were defeated by the little matter of an innings and 179 runs. As usual, the *Eastern Daily Press* was full of praise for the wicket, which was now being prepared by Leonard, the head gardener, but the paper also noted that Robinson was seriously ill. It turned out to be his last public appearance of any significance as he had less than two months to live.

The death and funeral of Lionel Robinson

Lionel Robinson died in his own bed on the 27 July 1922 aged only 55. His wife, Mary, survived him but the *Eastern Daily Press* reported that she had been an invalid for some years. The funeral took place at the All Saints Church, Old Buckenham, on the afternoon of Monday 31 July, 'in the presence of a very large gathering'. The body was carried from the Hall to the Church on a simple farm wagon, a mode of transport specifically requested by the deceased, and was met by the choir and the officiating clergy; the local vicar, the Rev Henry Anderson and the Rev R Jones, from the neighbouring parish of Banham. Psalm 121 was sung, followed by two of Lionel's favourite hymns, 'For All The Saints' and 'O God, Our Help In Ages Past', accompanied on the organ by Len Hart, who appears to have been the *renaissance* man of Old Buckenham. As six employees from the Estate bore the coffin down the aisle, the 'Nunc Dimittis' was chanted. The principal mourners were his wife, his two daughters and their husbands Colonel Brockbank and Major Evans, his brother, W.S., his nephew Lieutenant-Commander Lionel Frederick Robinson and William Clark, described as the 'deceased's partner and life-long friend'. There were many beautiful wreaths which showed the great respect in which Lionel was held. The *Norwich Mercury* reported that the silence and immobility of the crowd at the graveside was 'most impressive'; the grave itself, just to the north of the church, had been lined with evergreens by Lionel's garden staff. Robinson was unlucky with the weather to the last as it began to rain towards the end of the service – however the villagers were not deterred from paying their last respects. The *Eastern Daily Press* stated that Robinson had 'fully recognised the duties as well as the privileges of a landowner and will be sorely missed by all those resident on the estate, and by many others in the vicinity' whilst the *Norwich Mercury* finished its coverage by stating that 'Old Buckenham mourns the loss of a friend'. The overwhelming impression given by the local press is that, whilst Lionel Robinson may not have gained acceptance as a fellow 'toff' by the English aristocracy, his conduct as a squire had certainly passed muster with his villagers and, indeed, with the county of Norfolk. That none of the papers made any reference to mourners from the cricket world, one can only assume that, unless he had alienated every single cricketer (which is most unlikely), the funeral had intentionally been restricted to relatives and locals.

*Lionel Robinson memorial drinking fountain at Scotch College
(Scotch Collegian 1923)*

Lionel Robinson, as portrayed in his 1922 Scotch Collegian obituary.

The will of Lionel Robinson and the acceptance of his family into the nobility

Robinson left an estate of the gross value of £236,332 13s 3d, with net personalty of £133,952 16s 7d. He had last altered his will as late as 2 June last and probate had been granted to W.S. and to Bill Clark, who best knew his business. One hundred pounds was left to the Rev Anderson and his churchwardens, upon trust for investment so that the interest earned could be used to maintain the war memorial on Old Buckenham Green that Lionel had erected at his own expense. There were numerous bequests to his employees: John Oswald Kelloch (his cashier) received £500; William Boyce (his butler and an occasional cricketer) and George Beckett (his engineer) were each left £100; F Bramley and his wife (employees based in London), Annie Palmer (his head parlourmaid) and A.M.Hancock (his clerk) each received £50; Sergeant G Mea(d)cock (his commissionaire), A Warner (his head keeper) and A Cain (his chauffeur) were each granted £25; finally Harvey (his underkeeper), C Bunn (his gardener), Edith Wagg (his housemaid) and the loyal 'Squibs' (whose role was not specified) were rewarded with £10 apiece.

Once the minor bequests had been dealt with the bulk of his estate was divided up as follows: all his bloodstock, whether in training or based at his stud farms stationed at Old Buckenham, Newmarket or Stockbridge, which had been co-owned with his partner, William Clark, were left to Clark to dispose of as he saw fit; £1,500 plus his household and personal belongings, stores of consumables, carriages, motors and those horses which were not part of the bloodstock were left to his wife, again without condition; his two daughters, Viola Evans and 'Queenie' Brockbank each received £500 whilst each of their children inherited £100, as did his brother Gerald Henry Robinson, who was living in Melbourne; another brother still resident in Melbourne, Arthur Robinson, was left £200; his nephew, Lieutenant-Commander Lionel Frederick Robinson was granted £250 and given an annuity of £150, to be increased to £250 on the death of Lionel's widow; the Rev Henry Anderson was left £50 and there were small bequests and annuities to various relatives living in Australia. 'The residue of his property he left to his wife for life with remainder in trust in equal shares for his two daughters and their respective issue, with cross remainders.'

Robinson's younger daughter, 'Queenie', had two children. The elder Ann Marguerite Brockbank (1920-2009) in turn had two sons and a daughter from her marriage to Major John Pelham Mann. Her daughter, Celia Marguerite, married into the nobility, being wed in 1964 to George Willoughby Moke, who became the second Baron Norrie in 1977. The couple later divorced.

Queenie's son was John Myles Brockbank, known as Robin (1921-2006). He followed in his father's military footsteps and had a distinguished army career, being awarded the Military Cross in the Second World War and rising to the rank of Major-General. Robin also married into the gentry, his wife Gillian being the daughter of Sir Edmund Findlay, Bt., a Scottish politician and proprietor of The Scotsman newspaper. They had three sons and a daughter.

Lionel's older daughter, Viola, gave birth to two sons at Old Buckenham Hall. Ieuan Evans, born 1919, died at 17. The second son was Humphrey Evans, born two months after Lionel's death. In 1952, Humphrey married Cherry Drummond, later to become Lady Strange, and in 1966 he adopted the Drummond surname. Humphrey, also awarded a Military Cross in the Second World War, died in 2009. Eldest son, Adam, is the 17th Baron Strange whilst another son, also called Humphrey, works in the City. Their sister, Catherine Drummond-Herdman, is the owner of Megginch Castle in Perthshire. Thus, although Lionel himself behaved far too much like 'new money' to be accepted by the English aristocracy, his descendants, through both daughters, have met with no such rebuffs; this would doubtless have pleased their Papa immensely.

The South Norfolk Cricket Club
Mention was made in chapter five of the foundation of the South Norfolk Cricket Club by, amongst others, local schoolteacher Len Hart. The club started relatively slowly with only eight fixtures arranged in 1923, increasing to eleven in the1924 season and at least 30 in 1925. As well as playing a fairly full season of fixtures in Norfolk in that year, home and away, the club made a tour of Derbyshire in which they played six matches in six consecutive days. The highlight of the season was the hosting at Old Buckenham Hall of a fixture against Norfolk Club and Ground, in which the county players Geoffrey Stevens (with an unbeaten 82) and Walter

Everard Gates, bon viveur cricketer and record-breaking politician.
(Lafayette-National Portrait Gallery)

Beadsmoore (who took six for 40) ensured a heavy defeat for the home team. At the end of the season two brothers, Basil and Rodney Rought-Rought, made their first appearances for South Norfolk. Within a year both had been selected to play for Norfolk and, although both preferred to play for Brandon (their place of birth), they contributed significantly to the success of South Norfolk whenever they were available. The club also held social events off the field of play. Philip Yaxley reports that 'grand dances and lavish dinners' were held in Norwich and reports of golf tournaments also occur in the press.

The uncertainty about the medium-term future of the club caused by Robinson's death, was largely dispelled by the sale of the Old Buckenham Estate by Lionel's widow to Ernest Gates, a successful industrialist from Bradford who continued to permit the club to use the facilities during his short period as lord of the manor. When he died in 1925, the situation improved still further for the South Norfolk as his bibulous son, Everard, was not just a willing host but also an enthusiastic cricketer in his own right who was more than keen to turn out for the Club. Everard Gates is first spotted in the *Eastern Daily Press* as a cricketer in June 1924, when he turned out for L.W.J.Hart's XI but failed to trouble the scorers; however one of the first signs of his enthusiasm was his arrangement of a match between Old Buckenham Hall and Old Buckenham in June 1925. Hall won by 44 runs with Gates skippering and performing relatively well with both bat and ball, scoring 14 runs and taking three wickets. He then captained South Norfolk against the Gold Coast, a touring side, and managed to fit in a few more appearances during the 1925 season. A six-wicket haul against the Norwich General Post Office left him at the top of the bowling averages published in the *Eastern Daily Press* but his grand total of seven wickets at 8.00 contrasts starkly with the record of the second-placed Len Hart, who took no fewer than 95 wickets (at a cost of 10.39 apiece).

Gates at the helm of cricket in Old Buckenham
In 1926, and actively encouraged by Len Hart who put in the 'hard yards' as secretary behind the scenes, Gates began to emulate Lionel by bankrolling 'his' new club - with the notable difference that, whilst Robinson loved to play the bountiful host at Old Buckenham Hall, Gates was much more amenable to the concept of playing away from home, even participating in that year's tour[64] which was organised by Hart. At the start of the cricket season the *Eastern Daily Press* reported that the South Norfolk Club had secured the services of Burnett Wedlake Bullock, who had been on the ground staff at Surrey 'to assist in the cricket revival which Mr Everard Gates is organising amid the delightful surroundings familiar to many

---

64   Gates' behaviour on the tour in 1926 provided the first solid evidence of what was soon to become all too obvious; that he had some serious issues with alcohol. As an example, South Norfolk's heavy defeat by the Derbyshire club of Blackwell was attributed to the fact that Gates kept the team up until early in the morning, quaffing huge amounts of champagne in celebration of his birthday. To be fair to Gates, Philip Yaxley has pointed out that the other players of the South Norfolk Club, having been led to water, had a record of not refusing to drink. He states of the club's tours that 'the social side seemed as important as the cricket' and that the squad travelled in a vehicle known as the 'Beer Bus'.

Gates' XI v Leveson-Gower's XI, Old Buckenham, 1926. (Philip Yaxley)

distinguished cricketers in Mr Lionel Robinson's days'. Bullock, aged 30, had scored prolifically both for Surrey Club and Ground and for Surrey Seconds and had probably come to Gates' notice the previous year when he and Charles Daily struck 200 runs off the Norfolk attack in just 105 minutes as Surrey Seconds racked up 550 for five before declaring. It was further reported that the South Norfolk Club had arranged no fewer than 40 matches for the forthcoming season, with the two two-day games arranged against H.L.Simms' XI and H.D.G.Leveson-Gower's XI as part of 'Old Buckenham Hall Week' in July being the outstanding fixtures. When the time came to look back on the season, the *Eastern Daily Press* reported that South Norfolk had had a relatively successful season, but not one with which Lionel Robinson would have been satisfied. Although 17 matches were won, no fewer than ten were lost. Bullock more than justified his wages, scoring over 1,000 runs at an average of over 67 and taking 51 wickets at 12.29. As a batsman he received most support from the brothers Rought-Rought while the bowling was dominated by Hart, who took no fewer than 134 wickets at 10.26.

Old Buckenham Week was a rather complex affair with players coming and going and swapping sides in a seemingly random fashion. The home team were not South Norfolk, as one might have expected, but the Rudolph Ramblers, a side composed chiefly of past and present members of Magdalen College, Oxford. Their first match was against Harry Simms' XI, whose team included both Gates and Hart whilst the Ramblers were strengthened by Bullock and duly won. The Ramblers then took on South Norfolk in a one-day game. Gates joined the Ramblers' team but Hart and Bullock turned out for South Norfolk instead and the former's five-wicket haul meant a defeat for the Ramblers. A second loss was only narrowly avoided at the hands of H.D.G.Leveson-Gower's XI, who were 16 runs short with three wickets in hand when stumps were drawn. Gates again turned out for the Ramblers, being joined by Bullock, but Hart made it a hat-trick

South Norfolk CC at Blackwell, 1926. (Philip Yaxley)

South Norfolk CC 1920s.

of appearances against the Ramblers. The match was dominated by the Ramblers' GS Incledon-Webber who scored 130 (out of 198) in his first knock and took six for 44 in the first innings of Leveson-Gower's XI.

Alas, that early six-wicket haul against the 'Posties' flattered to deceive, and Everard Gates proved to be almost as inept a performer on the cricket pitch as his predecessor and his relatives. Unlike Lionel, he did put himself on to bowl quite regularly and managed to snaffle an occasional wicket or two[65] but his batting was every bit as mediocre as Robinson's; despite batting himself up and down the order he found making a double-figure

---

65   Gates' total haul of 26 wickets in 1926 were relatively expensive at 17.30 apiece.

score an almost impossible feat.

With South Norfolk playing a full season in 1926, Len Hart had no need to 'slum it' by continuing to play for the village team, or even to raise his own sides. South Norfolk and Old Buckenham had drifted far apart, with the former team playing cricket of a much higher standard, both in terms of skill and of social class, than the latter, who returned to the lowly level bottom-feeding that marked their existence before the arrival of Lionel Robinson. By 1928 their results were no longer appearing in the *Eastern Daily Press*, which suggests that they had temporarily ceased to exist. The South Norfolk League carried on until the early 1930s when it, too, folded.

Although results on the field of play were satisfactory in the following season, with 17 games out of a total of 30 being won, things seem to have started to go amiss with Gates' grandiose plans as early as this year. First, he lost the services of Burnett Bullock, who participated in the first few matches of the season but then inexplicably vanished. Second, there was a depressing report in the *Eastern Daily Press*: 'The Press Association states that the match arranged to be played at Old Buckenham Hall on August 29 and 30 between the New Zealanders and an eleven chosen by Mr Everard Gates has been cancelled.' Again, no reason was given but perhaps the possibility of running into the French actor Maurice Chevalier (apparently a regular visitor to Old Buckenham Hall at that time) was too much of a risk for the MCC to take. The sole high point was that the Hall pitch continued to impress, there being a reference in the press to a 'perfect wicket prepared by [groundsman] Harold Prince'. As regards individuals, the team continued to rely on the batting of the brothers Rought-Rought and the bowling of Rodney Rought-Rought and Len Hart. Gates himself took but seven expensive wickets and failed to score enough runs to merit inclusion in the batting averages. The 1928 season was very similar to the previous year in that there were 16 victories from 29 matches (as in the previous year there was no tour) and that the team's successes depended very much on the same three players as the previous year. To add to the similarity, the wicket was again described as 'plumb' and Gates failed to shine once more, averaging less than double figures with the bat.

In passing, it is of no little interest that the *Eastern Daily Press* made reference to 'the first cricket ground' laid down by Lionel Robinson during the 1928 season. Although it had long since ceased to function as a cricket ground, it was still serving as a sporting venue at that stage, being used to host the athletic sports meeting and fete organised by the Old Buckenham British Legion. It would again be noted as serving the same function in 1930. These brief references are the only explicit references surviving regarding Lionel's original ground at Old Buckenham.

The climax of the South Norfolk Club

Whether Gates continued to hold the whip hand or not, the standard of a typical cricketer who turned out for South Norfolk took a significant turn for the better in 1929. No fewer than 12 players who had represented Norfolk, or who would soon do so, turned out for South Norfolk. The

South Norfolk CC 1928. Front - R Warren, LWJ Hart, BW Rought-Rought,
Dr JH Owens, JJ Williams; middle - R Warren, W Dann, RC Rought-Rought,
EE Gates; back - EP Hogg, DC Rought-Rought.

quality of the opposition also improved which meant that the club won only 14 matches and lost as many as 11, including four on the tour, which had been resurrected after a gap of two years. Although the stalwart Rodney Rought-Rought was unable to play regularly,[66] his absence was partly compensated for by appearances by his baby brother Desmond and Harold Theobald, both county players in the making. With the standard improving, there was no chance that Gates would shine and his ten innings brought him just 65 runs. The year 1930 showed a similar pattern of South Norfolk putting out high quality elevens against tough opposition such as Felixstowe and the Gentlemen of Lincolnshire. Twelve matches were won and 14 lost, as Basil Rought-Rought and Thomas Carey made many runs, and Len Hart totally dominated the bowling, taking no fewer than 117 wickets without having significant support at the other end. Gates batted just four times and bowled not at all. For some reason, only a truncated list of fixtures was arranged for 1931, with a mere 23 matches played, as compared with the 37 arranged in the previous year. Both batting and bowling averages appear to be lower than usual, which might point to a deterioration in the quality of the wickets. Given that Gates was heading towards bankruptcy, it is not too hard to imagine that financial outlay on

---

66   The following paragraph was printed on page eight of the 4 May issue of *The Cricketer*, Volume X (1929): *'Fast Bowler Wanted. South Norfolk, who have arranged a most attractive Whitsun tour, require a fast bowler to take the place of the Norfolk bowler, R.C. Rought Rought, who is reading for an examination. Any player who can take part in the tour can be assured of a splendid week's cricket, for all the matches, the first of which is against Skegness on May 18, take place on first-class grounds. The Whit-Monday game is against Lincoln Lindum, followed by matches with Peterborough, Leicester Amateurs, Sleaford, and Kettering, the tour finishing on Friday, May 24. All hotel accommodation has been arranged, and there will be no travelling expenses from Norwich or Cambridge, as members of the South Norfolk club are providing cars. L.W.J. Hart, of Old Buckenham, Norfolk, will be very pleased to supply any further details.'*

the cricket square was not his highest priority; certainly South Norfolk's last game at Old Buckenham took place as early as 5 August. There was, however, no clue of the drastic events to come.

Decline and fall of Old Buckenham Hall and its cricket pitch

By the winter of 1931-2 it was clear that Gates was running short of funds. It would be all too easy to state that he had finally drunk himself into penury, aided by Len Hart and the rest of the South Norfolk Club, but times were hard and even the most hard-bitten and sober businessman might have found it troublesome to the point of ruination to maintain the upkeep of the cash-hungry Hall, let alone the cricket pitch. Gates was far from such a man and he had no option but to move out of the Hall into somewhere much more affordable and put the Hall itself up for sale. He arranged for Messrs Nicholas to publish a catalogue 'Old Buckenham Hall Sale 1932' and to hold an auction at the Royal Hotel, Norwich on 4 June.[67] In contrast to the 908 lots offered for sale by Prince Freddy in 1906, Everard Gates had his estate divided into just 36 lots. Special mention was made of the well-appointed cricket pavilion (with showers and lavatories, an office, a kitchen and a central tea-room), the collection of paintings and the stud farm, with its winter paddocks, large loose boxes and outbuildings. The Hall itself was described as having been rebuilt in 1911 by Messrs Cubitt from the designs of Detmar Blow and to have been further modernised in 1927 (a total of 29 telephones was noted). The economic situation globally meant that it was an inauspicious time to try and sell a large country house and Gates failed to find a buyer. *Kelly's Directory of Norfolk* for 1933 reports that the Hall was unoccupied and that, although Gates was listed as being one of the principal landowners in the parish of Old Buckenham, he did not appear to be living locally.

Faced with the loss of their picturesque ground and their superb wicket, which rarely received less than rave reviews, the South Norfolk Club behaved in a manner that can only be described as pusillanimous – essentially the club was wound up. Two brief tours, each of three matches, were arranged in 1932 and 1933, with five of the matches being played at Skegness and one at Sleaford. They were, however, very much a coda to the history of the club proper. It was notable that, during the mid and late 1930s, there were clubs representing East Norfolk, West Norfolk and North Norfolk; the absence of the 'fourth' club stood out. Perusal of the *Eastern Daily Press* suggests that no cricket at all was played at Old Buckenham between 1932 and 1935, but the village team came back to life (again) in 1936. The quality of the play was poor, with each Old Buckenham wicket scoring less than six runs on average. Interestingly, the press reported that some of the club's home matches were played at 'Old Buckenham Hall' which would seem to imply that those fixtures were played amid the slowly decaying wreck of Lionel's once-magnificent estate.

---

67   Gates had actually tried to sell Old Buckenham Hall once before, in April 1928; the catalogue describing that sale being positively threadbare compared to that issued for the sale of Prince Freddy's estate. Beyond the existence of this catalogue, there is little evidence that Gates was in financial difficulties as early as 1928.

When Gates finally managed to sell up in 1936 the new owner, Captain T.J.F.Sewell,[68] who was the headmaster of South Lodge Preparatory School in Lowestoft, converted the Hall at Old Buckenham into a boys' school; this opened in January 1937 with a total of 32 boys. A portion of the Estate was put up for auction at the Royal Hotel, Norwich, in August 1937 with yet another Old Buckenham Hall catalogue being printed.

The new Old Buckenham Hall School struggled through the war years but was beginning to flourish when, on 5 December 1952, a disastrous fire destroyed the grand house that Lionel had lavished so much of his wealth and pride upon. The school moved to Merton, near Watton, where fire struck again four years later, necessitating a further resettlement to its present home at Brettenham Hall in Suffolk.[69] Shortly after, Lionel's rustic thatched pavilion was transported to Brettenham where it still exists and the thatcher who had first roofed the building in 1911 returned nearly 50 years on to repeat his handiwork.

If Lionel Robinson's brash manner and conspicuous spending habits prevented him from gaining acceptance from the landed gentry, the reports of his funeral indicate that 'his' villagers held him in great esteem. Everard Gates was also a 'big spender' but his behaviour did not win the approval of the locals. Far from it; Barry Wilson, writing as late as 1977 which was 40 years after Gates sold and left, states that Everard was still remembered in Old Buckenham for his wild parties, complete with 'chorus girls' (who were presumably not there to accompany Maurice Chevalier's singing).

To be fair to Gates, he was not always the unreconstructed sot so unfondly remembered at Old Buckenham. Not only did he attain the rank of major in the Second World War but he had a not unsuccessful career as a politician. In 1929, while still resident at the Hall, he had been adopted as the Conservative Party candidate for the constituency of Deptford. He finished a distant second in what was a safe seat for Labour but conducted himself sufficiently impressively that, 11 years later, he was chosen to contest the seat of Middleton and Prestwick. Gates obtained 32,036 votes, which represented a Hoxha-esque 98.7 per cent share of the total and remains the record for a parliamentary by-election in the UK. The other 418 voters chose to support a certain F Haslam, who was representing the British Union of Fascists (BUF); Sir Oswald Mosley tried to campaign for Haslam but required police protection to escape a furious mob. In the next few days the BUF was declared illegal and its leaders were interned. Gates' bibulous past was clearly no hindrance to his acquiring a safe Conservative seat and may have been put down to youthful high spirits (he was still under 30 when he had to vacate Lionel's Hall). He continued to sit in Parliament until standing down in 1951 and lived to the ripe old age of 81, his liver seemingly undamaged.

---

68   Captain Sewell was the father of Donald Sewell, who was to become headmaster
      of Old Buckenham School in turn, and whose opinion on the origin of the soil
      in Lionel's pitches was given in chapter three.
69   The name of Old Buckenham Hall was retained, even after the relocation of
      the school.

Epilogue:
Robinson – 'new money' and cricket

There have been several examples of individuals with huge fortunes, recently acquired, who have followed Lionel in deciding to spend large amounts on cricket in one way or another. As well as the aforementioned Sir Julien Cahn, the names of the abrasive Kerry Packer and the disgraced Allen Stanford spring to mind.

Lionel and Sir Julien, though very different men, had much in common and were far removed from the profit driven megalomaniacs of more recent acquaintance. Both constructed their own grounds[70] and raised their own personal elevens who would play high quality matches in front of spectators who were admitted free. Cahn's biographer, Miranda Rijks, states: 'Cahn's cricket was the epitome of "country house cricket", although considerably more ambitious and competitive than any country house cricket seen up until then.' but she is clearly unaware of the story of Old Buckenham which was over before Cahn's tentative beginnings in 1923 but which was by no means eclipsed by the deeds of her grandfather. There were, however, significant differences between Lionel and Cahn. Although both were aware that they were personally inept as cricketers, only Lionel 'stood down' from playing in his own sides to avoid embarrassment. Cahn insisted on turning out for his own elevens; this led to him being described as the worst player to feature in first-class cricket and caused much awkwardness as his team mates and opponents had to collude in order to ensure that he at least got off the mark. It also led to moments of humiliation when Cahn came on to bowl for Rijks informs us that he purveyed such 'flighted filth' that the spectators would often jeer and he would occasionally respond by having the entire crowd evicted. Cahn also organised far more matches than Archie MacLaren arranged for Lionel; whilst Old Buckenham at its peak would never see more than 12 matches, Cahn's side often played 40 matches in a calendar year. To ensure that he had sufficient players on hand, Cahn found jobs for many of his players in his business empire.[71] Given that many of Cahn's cricketers were (sh) amateurs if not downright professionals one has to doubt whether his cricket can really be referred to as 'the epitome of "country house cricket"'; indeed, did it qualify as country house cricket at all? Finally, whilst nearly all of Lionel's matches were played at home, Cahn loved to travel and

---

70   Cahn's ground was at West Bridgford, near Nottingham.
71   Writing of the match between Cahn's Team and the New Zealanders of 1931, Peter Wynne-Thomas states that: 'Eight of the Cahn team were wholly or partially employed by Cahn in his furniture or allied businesses. More generally, he also writes that: 'Cahn *employed* (my emphasis) cricketers of all grades ...'

*Lionel Robinson's memorial in All Saints Church, Old Buckenham
(photo by Ron Brewer)*

*The Robinson tomb by the north door at Old Buckenham Church where
Lionel and his wife Mary are buried. (Tom Walshe)*

Old Buckenham Hall from the air. The cricket ground is to the far left, sightscreen visible in corner. (courtesy of Roger Wilson)

Old Buckenham Hall Ground 100 years on with modern pavilion and electronic scoreboard. Lionel's rustic thatched pavilion was sited to the right where the nets now stand. (Tom Walshe)

Robinson's second thatched pavilion, now at Old Buckenham Hall School, Brettenham in Suffolk. (Tom Walshe)

organised six overseas tours.

It is often thought that both Lionel and Cahn remained outsiders, prevented from being welcomed into the English cricketing establishment by being 'new money' and by being, either an irascible Australian (Lionel), or Jewish (Cahn). Certainly neither was invited to become a member of the MCC and it is clear that prejudice did a thorough job in curtailing Cahn's ambitions over the decade and a half in which he was active in the cricket world. That Lionel was also 'blackballed' by the establishment is a little harder to prove. He was bankrolling the 1912 Triangular Tournament within two years of making his first significant investment in cricket (the construction of his first ground) but subsequent events meant that any ambitions that he may have had to join the establishment were thwarted. The outbreak of the Great War ended any major tours after 1912;[72] it is just conceivable that, if war had been avoided, the MCC might have been seduced by Lionel's money every bit as much as the EWCB were by the apparent fortune of Stanford – on the other hand they might have pocketed his money and still withheld membership of their club. From what is known of Lionel, a thick-skinned colonial, it seems that he might not have been that bothered.

However, there remains the matter of the visit to Old Buckenham of the Australians in 1921, the like of which has never been repeated. In moments of doubt, the author had begun to wonder whether the existence of this fixture, so fantastic and prestigious a beast, can only be explained in terms of Lionel being at least partway 'accepted' by the establishment and permitted the match. But much more likely is the hypothesis, advanced in chapter six, that Lionel bypassed the MCC and the ABC altogether and used all his influence and money to insert his match into the tourists' schedule.

West entrance gates, Old Buckenham Hall, leading towards the cricket ground...
dilapidated but still standing despite Lionel's motor car incident.
Note also the innovative electric light portholes. (Tom Walshe)

---

72   The Australians were not scheduled to make their next tour until 1916 with the South Africans visiting in the following year.

Acknowledgements

Thanks for the original encouragement to write this book are due to David Jeater, who assured me that, in the light of his role of a financier of country house cricket to the highest level, Robinson's own utterly inept performances on the field of play did not disqualify him from being a suitable subject for the *Lives in Cricket* series.

Equally profuse thanks are due to Tom Walshe, a member of the Old Buckenham Cricket Club, who published an excellent article on Lionel in the *Eastern Daily Press* as far back as 2006, and who has contributed to the production of this volume in three ways. He has been kind enough to provide a highly thought-provoking Foreword and to offer his erudite comments on the manuscript, which were as helpful as one would expect from someone who is exceedingly well-informed about Lionel's personal life. He has also used his local knowledge to provide me with a huge variety of photographs and documents of great interest to a would-be biographer of Lionel and introduced me to Roger Wilson, the leading expert on the history of Old Buckenham who also leant me some valuable photographs. I have greatly enjoyed swapping ideas and developing theories with Tom.

When Tom and I first met he was already in contact with various interested parties in Australia and he provided me with the email addresses of Colin Riley, who has written a splendid article on Lionel Robinson in *The Yorker* magazine (the journal of the Melbourne Cricket Club Library); Bruce Brown and, most significantly, of Michael Robinson, the grandson of Lionel's brother Sir Arthur Robinson, allowing me the privilege of making contact with the last myself. Michael turned out to be the 'holy grail' of the whole affair, taking the trouble to fill in a number of troublesome gaps in our knowledge in a lengthy email and dealing frankly and knowledgeably with the matter of Lionel's parents and the timing of their marriage. I can pay Michael no higher compliment than to quote David Jeater's comment on seeing his email: 'In my experience it is very rare to contribute on that scale to an inquiry. Especially when he's not even a direct descendant.' Subsequently Michael provided copies of several documents which were of great value. Finally, during a visit to Britain, he was also generous enough to entertain Tom and myself to a splendid lunch in London, during which we had many profitable and interesting discussions in Lionel's character and motivation

Colin Riley, who used to live in Old Buckenham and now resides in Melbourne, and who retains an active interest in Lionel, and Bruce Brown, a former master at Scotch College, Melbourne, currently engaged in writing the Centenary History of the Scotch Old Boys ('With a keen but loving eye') that includes a chapter on 'The Remarkable Robinsons', have both provided valuable information on Lionel from their viewpoint 'down-under'. Intriguing theories about Lionel have been developed at long distance, courtesy of the internet.

Kevin Gates, the Research Officer of the Australian Racing Museum, has also provided valuable information on the deeds of horses owned by Lionel that were raced in Australia.

Michael Down is owed a vote of thanks for putting me in touch with Tom Walshe in the first place, for presenting me with a free copy of the book on the Hearne family and for allowing Tom and me access to the scrapbook of Archie MacLaren's son, Ian.

Roger Mann kindly provided numerous valuable photographs from his vast collection while Philip Yaxley provided some crucial pictures from his archive on Norfolk life; Keir Hounsome volunteered vital information on the South Norfolk Cricket League in particular and village cricket in 1920s Norfolk in general and also allowed me access to his copies of *The Cricketer* so that I might chase up references to Lionel that I discovered in Peter Wynne-Thomas' invaluable index to that periodical; Mike Davage offered moral support and was always able to put a Christian name to a set of initials.

The Library at Norwich Forum and the British Newspaper Library at Colindale both provided access to vital newspapers and their respective staffs are to be much thanked for their friendly and efficient help.

Thanks are also due to Rachel and Tomi Neaman-Pauk and to Howard and Susan Cottam-Davies for hosting me while I was staying in London to visit Colindale. Many thanks go to Kit Bartlett for proof-reading.

Bibliography

Books
David Rayvern Allen (ed), *Cricket's Silver Lining 1864-1914*, Guild Publishing, 1987
John Arlott (ed), *Cricket. The Great Captains*, Pelham Books Ltd, 1971
David Armstrong, *A Short History of Norfolk County Cricket*, The Larks Press, 1990
Warwick Armstrong, *The Art Of Cricket*, Methuen & Co, 1922
Philip Bailey (ed), *First-Class Cricket Matches: 1912* (and other years to 1921),
    ACS Publications, 2007 (and later years)
Philip Bailey, Philip Thorn and Peter Wynne-Thomas, *Who's Who of Cricketers*
    (Revised Edition), Hamlyn in association with ACS, 1993
Henry Blofeld, *The Packer Affair*, Wm Collins Sons & Co, 1978
Handasyde Buchanan (ed), *Great Cricket Matches*, Eyre & Spottiswode, 1962
Mike Davage, *Knights In Whites, Major Men*, Breckland Print, 2011
Stephen Dorril, *Black Shirt: Sir Oswald Mosley And British Fascism*, Viking, 2006
Michael Down, *Archie: A Biography of A.C. MacLaren*, George Allen and Unwin, 1981
Leslie Duckworth, *S.F. Barnes: Master Bowler*, Hutchinson, 1967
Patrick Ferriday, *Before The Lights Went Out. The 1912 Triangular Tournament*,
    Von Krumm Publishing, 2011
Peter Griffiths, *Complete First-Class Match List, Volume II: 1914/15-1944/45*,
    ACS Publications, 1997
Peter Griffiths and Peter Wynne-Thomas, *Complete First-Class Match List,
    Volume I: 1801-1914*, ACS Publications, 1996
Gideon Haigh, *The Big Ship: Warwick Armstrong and the Making of
    Modern Cricket*, Aurum Press, 2002
J.W. 'Jack' Hearne, *Wheelwrights to Wickets*, Boundary Books, 1996
Michael Home, *Spring Sowing,* Methuen & Co Ltd, 1946
John Kenworthy-Brown, Peter Reid, Michael Sayer and David Watkin,
    Burke's And Savill's Guide To Country Houses. Volume III. East Anglia,
    Burke's Peerage Ltd, 1981
David Lemmon, *Johnny Won't Hit Today*, George Allen & Unwin, 1983
David Lemmon, *Percy Chapman: A Biography*, Queen Anne Press, 1985
Jeremy Malies, *Great Characters From Cricket's Golden Age*, Robson Books, 2000
Christopher Martin-Jenkins (ed), *The Cricketer Book Of Cricket Eccentrics
    And Eccentric Behaviour*, 1985
Ronald Mason, *Jack Hobbs*, Hollis and Carter, 1960
Ronald Mason, *Warwick Armstrong's Australians*, Epworth Press, 1971
Leo McKinstry, *Jack Hobbs. England's Greatest Cricketer*, Yellow Jersey Press, 2011
Stephen Musk, *Michael Falcon: Norfolk's Gentleman Cricketer*, ACS, 2010
Horrie Panks and Roger Wilson, *Sporting Life Of Old Buckenham*,
    privately printed, 1990s
Roland Perry, *Bradman's Invincibles. The Story of the 1948 Ashes Tour*,
    Aurum Press, 2009
Peter Richardson, *Collins House Financiers. William Baillieu, Lionel Robinson
    and Frances Govett*, manuscript.
Miranda Rijks, *The Eccentric Entrepreneur: A Biography of Sir Julien Cahn Bt.
    (1882-1944)*, The History Press, 2008
William Sydney Robinson, *If I Remember Rightly*, FW Cheshire, 1967
Donald Sewell, *A History of Old Buckenham Hall School*, OBHS, 1992
EHD Sewell, *The Log of a Sportsman*, T Fisher Unwin, 1923
AA Thomson, *Cricket Bouquet*, Museum Press Ltd, 1960
Peter Wynne-Thomas, *The Complete History Of Cricket Tours At Home and Abroad*,
    Hamlyn, 1989
Peter Wynne-Thomas, *Sir Julien Cahn's Team: 1923 To 1941*, ACS, 1994

Philip Yaxley, *Looking Back at Norfolk Cricket*, Nostalgia Publications, 1997
Peter Yule, *William Lawrence Baillieu: Founder Of Australia's Greatest
    Business Empire*, Hardie Grant Books, 2012

Newspapers
*The Adelaide Advertiser, The Adelaide Chronicle, The Adelaide Register,
The Argus (Melbourne), The Australian, The Barrier Miner (Broken Hill),
The Bathurst Times (NSW), The Daily Chronicle, The Daily Express,
The Daily News (Perth), The Daily Telegraph, The Eastern Daily Press,
The Eastern Evening News, The Kalgoorlie Miner, The Launceston Examiner,
The Manchester Guardian, The Melbourne Sun, The Morning Post,
The Norfolk Chronicle and Norwich Gazette, The Norwich Mercury,
Port Macquarie News and Hastings River Advocate,
The Queensland Figaro (Brisbane), The Richmond River Herald, The Sunday Times,
The Sunday Times (Perth),The Times, The West Australian (Perth),
The Yarmouth Mercury*

Periodicals and annuals
The Cricketer magazine, *Norfolk County Cricket Club* annual reports, *Norfolk Fair*
magazine, *The Scotch Collegian* periodical, *Wisden Cricketers' Almanack* annuals

Censuses
Censuses for 1901 and 1911

Websites
http://en.wikipedia.org/wiki/London_Stock_Exchange
http://oldbuckenham.blogspot.com - November 2008, 'Our village sign', February
2009, 'Snapshots of past', and February 2011, 'Cricket in Old Buckenham'.
http://www.adb.online.anu.edu.au/biogs/A110438b.htm
http://www.britishlistedbuildings.co.uk/en-495549-war-memorial-old-buckenham
http://www.roll-of-honour.com/Norfolk/OldBuckenham.html
www.cricketarchive.com
www.cricinfo.com

Directories
Kelly's Directory Of Norfolk, 1912, 1916, and *1933,* Kelly's Directories Ltd

Saleroom catalogues
Old Buckenham Hall Catalogue 1906, Pettitt & Cox
Old Buckenham Hall Catalogue 1928, Wood & Foxlow
Old Buckenham Hall Sale 1932, Messrs Nicholas
Old Buckenham - Kitchen gardens, garage and woodlands and Downmere Farm 1937.

Appendix one
Lionel Robinson's XI in first-class cricket

Played six: Won two, Drawn four.

For L.Robinson's XI

Highest team score: 362-8 d v Australian Imperial Forces, 1919

Lowest team score: 147 v Oxford University 1914
and v Australian Imperial Forces, 1919

Highest individual score: Sir T.C.O'Brien 111 v Oxford University, 1914

Best bowling return: S.F.Barnes 23.3-4-88-7 v J.R.Mason's XI, 1913

For opponents:

Highest team score: 339 by Oxford University, 1914

Lowest team score: 66 by South Africans, 1912

Highest individual score: 96* E.L.Kidd for Cambridge University, 1913

Best bowling return: S.J.Pegler 20-3-45-6 for South Africans, 1912

Match scores in brief:

5, 6 and 7 September 1912 . **L.Robinson's XI** 153 (S.J.Pegler 6-45) and 255 (E.H.Hendren 80, S.J.Pegler 5-75): **South Africans** 151 (M.Falcon 6-47) and 66 (F.A.Tarrant 5-8, H.L.Simms 5-24). **L.Robinson's XI won by 191 runs.**

3, 4 and 5 July 1913. (Twelve a side) **L.Robinson's XII** 195 (B.J.T.Bosanquet 86, Hon H.G.H.Mulholland 4-28, Hon F.S.G.Calthorpe 4-20) and 307 (B.J.T.Bosanquet 55, A.C.MacLaren 50*): **Cambridge University** 139 (M.Falcon 5-55, S.J.Pegler 4-71) and 321 (E.L.Kidd 96*, R.D.Evans 70, R.O.Schwarz 5-88, G.G.Napier 4-90). **L.Robinson's XII won by 42 runs.**

1, 2 and 3 September 1913. **L.Robinson's XI** 236-7dec (B.J.T.Bosanquet 79, D.W.Carr 5-41) and 71-5: **J.R.Mason's XI** 216 (E.Humphrey 69, S.F.Barnes 7-88). **Match drawn.** *Rain prevented play on the first day.*

2, 3 and 4 July 1914. **Oxford University** 339 (D.J.Knight 82, M.Howell 50, B.G.von B.Melle 54, S.J.Pegler 7-113): **L.Robinson's XI** 147 (Sir T.C.O'Brien 90, C.E.S.Rucker 5-26) and following on, 311-7 (Sir T.C.O'Brien 111, J.C.W.MacBryan 65, B.J.T.Bosanquet 59). **Match drawn.**

14, 15 and 16 May 1919. (Twelve a side) **L.Robinson's XII** 147 (C.T.Docker 5-34) and 362-8d (H.T.W.Hardinge 72, G.D.Hough 87*): **Australian Imperial Forces** 227 (H.L.Collins 87, S.J.Pegler 5-54) and 274-9 (.J.M.Taylor

66, C.B.Willis 57, J.W.H.T.Douglas 4-80). **Match drawn.** *A.I.F. were left 283 to win in 225 minutes but could not sustain the scoring rate needed.*

4, 5 and 6 May 1921. **Australians** 136 (W.W.Armstrong 51*, J.W.H.T.Douglas 6-64) and 25-1: **L.Robinson's XI** 256-7d (J.B.Hobbs 85, V.W.C.Jupp 59*, E.A.McDonald 4-62). **Match drawn.** *Rain curtailed play on all three days.*

Averages in first-class games:

M	I	NO	HS	R	Ave	100	50	0Ct/St	O	M	R	WAve	BB	5w
SF Barnes	1	1	1	13*	13	-	-	-	-	-	23.3	4	88	7	12.57	7-88	1
BJT Bosanquet***	4	8	-	86	292	36.50	-	4	1	1	-	-	-	-	-	-
JL Bryan	1	2	-	18	27	13.50	-	-	-	-	-	-	-	-	-	-
CP Buckenham	1	1	-	6	6	6.00	-	-	-	-	14	4	32	-	-	-	-
APF Chapman	1	1	-	0	0	0.00	-	-	1	1	-	-	-	-	-	-
JWFA Crawfurd	1	2	-	15	24	12.00	-	-	-	-	6	1	12	1	12.00	1-12	-
H Dean	1	1	1	2*	2	-	-	-	-	-	5	2	9	1	9.00	1-9	-
JWHT Douglas	2	3	1	41*	54	27.00	-	-	-	1	68.5	12	227	13	17.46	6-64	1
AJ Evans	1	2	-	48	55	27.50	-	-	-	1	10	3	38	-	-	-	-
M Falcon*	2	4	-	29	59	14.75	-	-	-	1	45	9	181	11	16.45	6-47	2
PGH Fender	1	1	-	10	10	10.00	-	-	-	1	-	-	-	-	-	-
GN Foster	1	2	-	25	27	13.50	-	-	-	1	-	-	-	-	-	-
EJ Fulcher	3	6	-	31	97	16.17	-	-	-	1	11	0	59	-	-	-	-
CH Gibson	1	1	-	1	1	1.00	-	-	-	-	25	11	34	4	8.50	3-33	-
G Gunn	1	2	1	41	76	76.00	-	-	-	-	-	-	-	-	-	-
HTW Hardinge	1	2	-	72	81	40.50	-	1	-	1	-	-	-	-	-	-
EH Hendren	3	5	1	80	163	40.75	-	1	-	2	-	-	-	-	-	-
JB Hobbs	1	1	1	85*	85	-	-	1	-	-	-	-	-	-	-	-
GWV Hopley	1	2	-	29	42	42.00	-	-	-	1	-	-	-	-	-	-
GD Hough	1	2	2	87*	117	-	-	1	-	-	-	-	-	-	-	-
JC Hubble	1	2	-	34	35	17.50	-	-	-	2	-	-	-	-	-	-
A Jacques	1	2	1	1*	1	1.00	-	-	1	-	-	-	-	-	-	-
PR Johnson	1	2	-	44	83	41.50	-	-	-	-	-	-	-	-	-	-
VWC Jupp	1	1	1	59*	59	-	-	1	-	1	2	0	19	-	-	-	-
AS Kennedy	1	1	-	0	0	0.00	-	-	1	2	23.3	4	72	1	76.00	1-36	-
EL Kidd	1	2	-	4	8	4.00	-	-	-	1	-	-	-	-	-	-
DJ Knight	1	1	-	1	1	1.00	-	-	-	2	-	-	-	-	-	-
AH Lang	1	2	-	9	9	4.50	-	-	1	1	-	-	-	-	-	-
JCW MacBryan	1	2	-	65	80	40.00	-	1	-	-	-	-	-	-	-	-
KR McCloughin	1	2	-	21	21	10.50	-	-	1	-	10	2	32	-	-	-	-
CD McIver	1	2	-	35	53	26.50	-	-	-	-	-	-	-	-	-	-
AC MacLaren*	3	4	2	50*	76	38.00	-	1	1	1	-	-	-	-	-	-
JR Mason*	1	1	-	18	18	18.00	-	-	-	-	-	-	-	-	-	-
RV Minnett	1	2	1	8*	8	8.00	-	-	1	1	-	-	-	-	-	-
LJ Moon	1	2	-	12	15	7.50	-	-	-	2/1	-	-	-	-	-	-
OC Mordaunt	1	2	1	1*	1	1.00	-	-	1	-	12	0	48	1	48.00	1-48	-
GG Napier	1	2	-	17	19	9.50	-	-	-	-	20	2	90	4	22.50	4-90	-
TC O'Brien	1	2	-	111	201	100.50	1	1	-	-	-	-	-	-	-	-
SJ Pegler	4	5	1	25	45	11.25	-	-	-	2	99.4	15	350	19	18.42	7-113	2
RO Schwarz	3	4	1	8	13	4.33	-	-	1	3	47.4	5	190	8	23.75	5-88	1
J Sharp	1	2	-	39	46	23.00	-	-	-	-	-	-	-	-	-	-
HL Simms	1	2	-	23	31	15.50	-	-	-	1	15	1	58	6	9.67	5-24	1
GA Stevens	1	2	-	14	25	12.50	-	-	-	3	-	-	-	-	-	-
FA Tarrant	2	3	-	49	85	28.33	-	-	-	2	32	12	77	8	9.63	5-8	1
HW Taylor	1	2	-	19	35	17.50	-	-	-	-	-	-	-	-	-	-

LHW Troughton	1	2	-	48	52	26.00	-	-	-	-	-	-	-	-	-	-	-
NC Tufnell	1	2	-	1	1	0.50	-	-	1	1	-	-	-	-	-	-	-
JC White	1	1	-	0	0	0.00	-	-	1	1	8	2	20	-	-	-	-
GEC Wood	2	3	-	2	2	0.67	-	-	2	4/1	-	-	-	-	-	-	-
FE Woolley	1	2	-	14	18	9.00	-	-	-	2	51	9	125	5	25.00	3-60	-
extras/RO/sub ct	-	-	-	-	168	-	-	-	-	1	-	-	133	2	-	-	-
TOTAL	**68**	**113**	**17**	**111**	**2440**	**25.42**	**1**	**12**	**14**	**44/2**	**529.1**	**98**	**1894**	**91**	**20.81**	**7-88**	**9**

The matches against Cambridge University and the AIF were XII-a-side. An asterisk indicates an appearance as skipper.

Appendix two
What's in a name?

It is irritating that teams raised by Robinson from his rural base did not always appear bearing his name; many of his elevens are referred to in the Norfolk press as 'Old Buckenham' or 'Old Buckenham Hall'. Nearly all of the teams whose matches were awarded first-class status went by the name of 'L Robinson's XI' but the nomenclature of other elevens with which Robinson was involved seems at times to be devoid of rhyme and reason. The village club that existed prior to the arrival of Robinson and turned out for routine Saturday games against local opposition was referred to in the press as 'Old Buckenham' and the first variation appears in the final fixture of 1909, when the side who played in the only two-day match of that year was labelled by the papers as 'L Robinson's XI'. In the following year, the majority of the games were village affairs and continued to be played under the title of 'Old Buckenham' whilst the label of 'L Robinson's XI' tended to be reserved for the two-day matches and the more important one-day matches.[73] If this would tend to suggest a simple picture in which the label of 'Old Buckenham' was for less important games, with the sponsor's name reserved for the prestigious matches then the nomenclature seen in 1911 properly queers the pitch. Whilst seven games were played as 'Old Buckenham' and five as 'L Robinson's XI', six were played under the new label of 'Old Buckenham Hall'. Inspection of the lists of players involved reveals that plain 'Old Buckenham' no longer automatically denoted a team made up largely of cricketers with a strong connection to the old village side – conversely humble locals often appeared for the theoretically senior 'L Robinson's XI'. The matches played by elevens with the novel title were seemingly inseparable in status from those played by 'L Robinson's XI'; for instance, the team representing 'Hall' (to which the new name was frequently abbreviated) against A Norfolk XI that year featured no less than eight players with first-class experience and was as powerful a side as any that Robinson had so far fielded.

Mercifully, some sort of logic appears to have been employed in 1912, in that the most important matches were contested by 'L Robinson's XI' and the minor Saturday friendlies were played by 'Hall'. (The village side of 'Old Buckenham', as such, had vanished by this point.). Unfortunately, this scheme fails to allow for the significant number of two-day fixtures which fall between two stools in that they are undoubtedly important but are certainly not of first-class status; as one might have feared there has been

---

73   One highly notable departure has been referred to in chapter two when the Yarmouth Conservative Club turned up to play Old Buckenham and found themselves playing against a team containing no fewer than six players with first-class experience. Unsurprisingly, they subsided by a little matter of 300 runs. Lionel, who was playing, would have loved every minute.

considerable inconsistency in the nomenclature of these intermediate sides. In some cases the contemporary press refers to a particular side both as 'Hall' and as 'L Robinson's XI' whilst the fixture against the MCC on the first two days in July, 1912, is listed in Cricket Archive as being against 'L Robinson's XI' but appears in the *Eastern Daily Press* as being contested by 'Hall'. In at least one game (against the Oxford University Authentics), which the Norfolk press lists under the 'junior' title, the side contained no fewer than four players with Test experience. This side was not greatly inferior to some of the teams that turned out for 'L Robinson's XI' in first-class games and makes a mockery of the proposal that the label of 'Hall' automatically denotes a less prestigious fixture. The nomenclature in 1913 was similar to that in 1912 but the picture changed again in 1914 when all six matches that took place were played as 'Old Buckenham Hall'.

After the Great War an independent village cricket club reformed and reclaimed the title of 'Old Buckenham'; what few matches that were bankrolled by Robinson continued to be played under his name or as 'Hall'. The leading cricketer in the village team, L.W.J.Hart, also raised an eponymous eleven on numerous occasions, starting in 1919; some villagers played in those teams too but Hart's elevens generally consisted of a better class of player than the humble villagers.

In view of the not always clear-cut differences between 'L Robinson's XI', 'L.W.J.Hart's XI', 'Old Buckenham Hall' and 'Old Buckenham' and the huge variation in the standard in the games played under the various titles, it does not seem in the slightest bit valid to draw up a set of averages for those games which were not deemed to be of first-class standard. Nor, indeed, are details always complete for matches involving the village side.

After Robinson's death, Old Buckenham continued to host the home games of several teams with overlapping identities. The village side and 'L.W.J.Hart's XI' retained their relative places in the pecking order while the slot for the most socially prestigious team was occupied by the newly-formed 'South Norfolk Club', described in chapters five and seven, who played friendlies of high quality at Old Buckenham Hall and who also started to organise tours in 1925. Other players than Hart did occasionally find themselves turning out for sides other than their regular eleven; for one game in 1924 'South Norfolk' were so short that they were forced to enlist the services of no fewer than five of the village cricketers to field a complete eleven. By 1926, however, the South Norfolk club had moved so far from the village side, both in terms of the standard of cricket that they played and of their social class, that they were now completely distinct entities.

For those not familiar with the geography of Norfolk, it is probably best to make it clear that Old Buckenham should not be confused with New Buckenham, Buckenham & Hassingham or Buckenham Tofts, all of which had their own cricket teams. In the period in which Robinson was active, the scores of three games, one each involving 'Buckenham', 'Buckenham Hall' and 'Buckenham Hall Estate', appeared in the *Eastern Daily Press*. Not one of the cricketers who turned out for these sides played in any team that can be located to Old Buckenham and I have not considered them further.

Index

A page number in bold indicates an illustration.